A SMALL KEY
CAN OPEN A LARGE DOOR

THE ROJAVA REVOLUTION

edited by strangers in a tangled wilderness

A Small Key Can Open A Large Door: The Rojava Revolution
edited by Strangers In A Tangled Wilderness

ISBN: 978-1-938660-17-7

Published in the United States by Strangers In A Tangled Wilderness, an
imprint of Combustion Books.
www.tangledwilderness.org
www.combustionbooks.org

Cover image by: seven resist, disorder rebel store berlin

Contents

A note from one of the many editors:

The book you're holding came together in fragments. Bits of translation came to us directly across the ocean and across the embargo lines or were posted to websites and listservs. We've done our best to stitch these stories and essays together for you, so that you and we both might better understand the bold social experiment and revolution that's happening right now in Rojava. Only human, I'm certain we've failed in places. Some pieces came to us without dates or stripped of their full context—still, we find them compelling and include them.

For the most part, we've left translations intact with their idiosyncrasies in grammar and form. A few transliterations have been regularized.

Acknowledgements:

A book like this is the combined effort of so many people. The editors would like to thank all the contributors who have offered their work to this enterprise. We are of course indebted to all the translators, especially our comrades in Istanbul. We would also like to thank the good people at Rojava News, The Kurdish Question, New Compass, and the Mesopotamian Academy in Rojava for all of their great writings and for providing background information on the issues surrounding this historic event. The editors would like to thank all the comrades in the US who supported this project and especially the group Rojava Solidarity NYC. Lastly, we would like to thank the people of Rojava for providing us with an inspiring example to struggle and strive for. It is for them that this book has been written. Long live the Rojava Revolution!

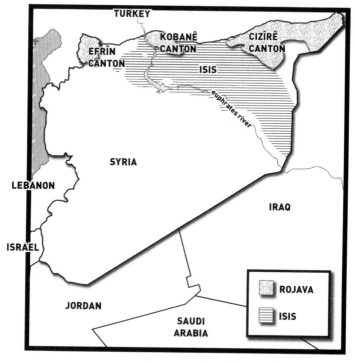

map is current as of November, 2014

Rojava:
Facts at a Glance

Name: "Rojava" is a word that means both "West" and "Sunset" in Kurdish. Each canton has its own anthem and flag.

Geography: Rojava lies in the northern part of Syria and the western part of Kurdistan. The area stretches over 1,437 square miles (making it a bit bigger than Rhode Island), and it is home to a total of 380 cities, towns, and villages.

Population: At the start of the Syrian civil war, Rojava was home to nearly 3.5 million people. Now, it is home to a little over 2.5 million (roughly twice the population of Rhode Island). Nearly a million people have fled, many to refugee camps in Turkey and Iraq. The most populous city in Rojava is Qamişlo (Cizîrê Canton), with more than 400,000 people.

Economics: Rojava's major economic resource is oil. The region produces about 40,000 barrels of crude oil a day. All Syrian refineries were located in the south of the country, so Rojava has had to build its own DIY refinery. Before the war there were some industries, namely concrete production sites and metal foundries, but the production from these industries has been disrupted by the civil war. Rojava is considered the breadbasket of Syria, cradled where it is between the Tigris and Euphrates rivers. The region major agricultural products are sheep, grain, and cotton. It was the only agricultural region in Syria to have a thriving export business prior to the war and the resulting embargo.

Military: The main fighting force of Rojava is a volunteer militias (namely the YPG and YPJ). The YPG/YPJ have a combined forced of 40,000 lightly-armed fighters. Most of the weapons are light firearms combined with Russian-made lightweight rocket launchers. They have also repurposed about 40 garbage trucks and other heavy trucks into armored personnel carriers. They have no aircraft.

Political Structure: Rojava is made up of three autonomous but confederated "cantons." These cantons are not geographically contiguous. The decisionmaking structure is composed of various councils. The average size of neighborhood councils is 30-150 families. A city district / village council is made up of 5-17 neighborhood councils (along with worker, non-profit, and religious councils). City district councils elect two representatives to the city council (one man and one woman). They also elect security and YPG/YPJ militias.

This introduction was written by some of this book's editors, in December 2014.

Introduction

A mountain river has many bends.
—From a Kurdish folk song

IT IS NEARLY AN IMPOSSIBLE TASK TO CHART THE BENDS AND tributaries of one of the world's longest running contemporary resistance movements—a one-hundred-and-fifty-year-old struggle that stretches from the opulence of the Ottoman Empire to today's bloody civil wars in Syria and Iraq. Books could be and have been written about the history, resistance, and hope for freedom of more than twenty-five million Kurds scattered across four belligerent and oppressive nation states. This slim volume is not a comprehensive history of this complex people and their enduring struggle, nor is it an essay on the Machiavellian geopolitics that have kept tens of millions of people oppressed for generations. This book is a bridge—between us radicals in the West, who have become cynical to the idea that anything can really change, and those who have dared an experiment in freedom in one of the most dangerous parts of the world against enemies so absurdly repressive and savage they seem to have come from a Hollywood script. We need some context to truly understand the words and ideas of the rebels of Rojava, else we can be easily seduced by over-simplifications and distortions—like the claims that the struggle in Rojava is a replay of the Spanish Revolution, or that it is a sophisticated public relations makeover for a Maoist national liberation struggle. These misunderstandings are not uniquely held by radicals—even the US government seems confused, the state department has various Rojavan groups on the terrorist watch list while at the same time the pentagon calls Kurdish fighters dangerous and illegal terrorists.

With so much misinformation and confusion about this little understood struggle, it is too easy for radicals to simply look the other way, admitting there is so much we don't know and understand. In today's world of stifling state and corporate control it would be a mistake and a betrayal of solidarity to ignore the struggles of this obscure region of northern Syria now called Rojava. To inspire our own work at home, we need to hear from those creating fragile and imperfect oases of freedom. The people risking their lives in the rubble of Kobanî need our support not only to resist the reactionary fanatic butchers that seek to kill every one of them but also as they try to create a stateless society based on ideals of freedom and equality.

The Kurds are an ethnically non-Arab group in the Middle East. Twenty-eight million of them inhabit a region known as Kurdistan, which spans adjacent areas of Syria, Turkey, Iran, and Iraq. By ethnicity and language, the Kurdish people are closer to Persians than they are to other peoples in the region. In ancient times Kurdish city-states were conquered and subjugated by Persians, Romans, and Arab invaders. All of these conquerors struggled to subdue the Kurds, often remarking on the Kurd's "stubborn demand of autonomy" (Xenophone). By the time of the rise of the Ottoman Empire in the 1500s, the Kurds had secured some autonomy through a string of independent principalities stretching from Syria to Iraq. The Ottomans left them alone for the most part until the beginning of the 19th century, when a number of bloody battles were fought to bring the independent areas under the control of Constantinople. The first major 19th century Kurdish uprising, Badr Khan Beg, took place in 1847. The Ottomans crushed this and subsequent uprisings, but the demand for Kurdish independence continued throughout the rest of the century.

At the end of World War I, the constitutional monarchist party of Turkey, the "Young Turks," began a systematic ethnic cleansing of the Kurds and, more infamously, the Armenians. From 1916 to 1918 the Young Turks forcibly deported 700,000 Kurds, more than half of them dying during the brutal process. On August 10, 1920, after the conclusion of World War I, the defeated Ottomans were compelled to sign the Treaty of Sèvres. The treaty split up the Ottoman empire, at the time dubbed "the sick man of the Bosphorus," into a number of independent non-Turkish states, which were to include an independent Kurdistan. But in 1922 the Turkish national movement, led by Mustafa Kemal Ataturk, a vehement Turkish nationalist and military officer, won the War of Independence and abolished the sultanate. This violent change of regimes forced England and the other allied powers to renegotiate the terms of the treaty with the fledgling nationalist state of Turkey. The Treaty of Sèvres was scrapped, and a new treaty, the Treaty of Lausanne, was signed by Ataturk and his nationalist congress July 24,, 1923. The Treaty of Lausanne gave Kurdistan back to Turkey, failing to even recognize that the Kurds existed. That same year, Ataturk decreed some 65 laws aimed at destroying Kurdish identity: renaming them "Mountain Turks;" outlawing public use of the Kurdish language; making Kurdish celebrations illegal; forcibly changing Kurdish names of streets, villages, businesses, etc. to "proper Turkish" names; confiscating huge tracts of Kurdish communal lands; seizing Kurdish community funds; eliminating all Kurdish or Kurd-sympathetic organizations or political parties; and so on. The few years of hope following the Treaty of Sèvres slipped into many decades of brutal state repression.

Iraq, Iran, and Syria, in which there were sizable Kurdish populations, also sought to keep the Kurds subjugated. The end of World War I simply switched Ottoman imperial oppression of the Kurds to the more systematic oppression of four authoritarian nation states, all of which had been either created or militarily propped up by the major allied victors of WWI as their protectorates.

Today's Syria was established as a French Colonial Mandate after the dismembering of the Ottoman Empire. At the time of the signing of the Treaty of Lausanne, 18% of people living in the French Mandate identified as Kurdish, making them the largest minority in the colony. After a number of failed uprisings by Syrian Arabs, the French adopted a divide-and-conquer strategy. They filled their colonial armies with Kurds, Christians, Druze, and other ethnic minorities and gave significant governing powers to Kurdish regional tribal leaders. When

Syria gained independence from France in 1946 it quickly attacked its "internal enemies." Close to 200,000 Kurds had their identity papers taken away and were declared stateless, allowing the new Syrian Republic to seize their land and property and to conscript them into forced labor. The new Arab-controlled republic changed all the names of Kurdish towns and resettled Arab Bedouins into most of the Kurd villages and towns to serve as police. In the first decades after independence, Kurdish organizations and customs were prohibited, and thousands of Kurdish political and tribal leaders were arrested. In 1973, Syrian officials decided to create an Arab corridor along the Turkish border and displaced about 150,000 Kurds without compensation. The 1980s and 90s saw periodic flare-ups of Kurdish demands for recognition of their culture and civil rights, which were often met with deadly interventions by the Syrian police or, in some cases, the army. Despite the systematic neglect and abuse of the Kurds within its own borders, Syria became an important training base and refuge for the Turkish PKK—a Marxist-Leninist organization dedicated to securing rights for the Kurds in Turkey—until the 1990s. Syria was playing a game of "my enemy's enemy is my friend" against Turkey, a policy that set the stage for the current events in Rojava.

In Iraq, the Kurdish situation was similarly cruel, though there it was the British who were the primary architects of their suffering, modern Iraq having been created as a result of the Sykes-Picot Agreement of WWI. The treaty of Lausanne effectively torpedoed Kurdish hopes for independence in Northern Iraq, and so the Kurds began a protracted campaign of armed struggle against their new British overseers. The British used aerial bombardments and punitive village burnings in order to

crush the ongoing Kurdish revolts in the Northeast of Iraq. After putting down three unsuccessful but very bloody revolts,
the British formally transferred control of Iraqi Kurdistan to
the newly formed Kingdom of Iraq, which functioned as a
British puppet state until a series of military coups eventually
elevated the Ba'ath party to power in 1968. The Kurds continued to struggle against the various Iraqi military regimes, both
militarily and politically. In 1946 they formed first the Kurdish Democratic Party and later, in 1975, the Patriotic Union
of Kurdistan. Eventually finding themselves in an uneasy truce
with the Ba'ath party in the early 70s, Iraqi Kurds experienced a
few brief years of relative calm before Saddam Hussein came to
power in 1979. Almost immediately, Saddam entered into the
decade-long Iran-Iraq war, during which he brought particular
brutality down onto the Iraqi Kurds because he believed they
were not sufficiently Iraqi and thus implicitly supported Iran. In
the al-Anfal Campaign of 1986-89 alone, between 100,000 and
200,000 Kurdish civilians were massacred with chemical weapons and in concentration camps. The war would end in a draw,
but Iraq would not stay out of conflict for long; it was invaded
by the United States and its NATO allies first in 1990 and then
again in 2003. The Kurds would use both of these conflicts to
leverage as much advantage as possible, which ultimately led
to the establishment of the Kurdistan Regional Government
(KRG) in 1991 and its de jure independence in 2005.

In Iran, Kurdish dreams of autonomy after generations of
Persian and Ottoman oppression started before World War I
during Iran's 1906 Constitutional Revolution. The new constitution guaranteed many rights but did not explicitly mention
ethnicity, so there were no specific rights protecting the Kurds

and their culture. Between 1906 and 1925, Kurds created a number of powerful political and civic organizations to support Kurdish rights and development in Iran. By 1924, there were dozens of Kurdish newspapers, three radio stations, and half a dozen political parties. In 1925, after oil was discovered in the country, the Shah seized power with backing of the West (namely the UK and US). Though the Shah gave lip service to the constitution of 1906, he started a Persianification campaign against the numerous minorities inside Iran, including the Kurds. This resulted in all-too-familiar Kurdish mass displacements, disappearances of civic and political leaders, prohibition of Kurdish language and culture, and military occupation of Kurdish regions. The 1979 Khomeini Revolution overthrew the despotic Shah regime but did not improve the life of Kurds. The new fundamentalist regime accelerated the nationalization process with laws and actions targeted against the Kurds and their culture. One of the first acts of the new regime was to launch a series of punishing military assaults to wrest away Kurdish control of the north. For six long bloody years, Iran put down Kurdish autonomy and resistance. In the early 2000s a new resistance group, J-Pak, strongly associated with the PKK, started a military campaign against the Iranian state, resulting a new round of state assaults on Kurdish villages. This time Iran added assassinations of Kurds in exile to their tools of repression. The US and Europe remained mostly silent on the repression of the Kurds, focusing their support on reform-minded Iranians instead of independence-minded Kurds, mostly in deference to Turkey. At the same time, Turkey has shared intelligence (and perhaps joint military interventions) with Iran and vice-versa to stop Kurdish resistance.

The repression of the Kurdish people in the four nation states of Turkey, Syria, Iraq, and Iran follow a nearly identical pattern involving mass deportations, outlawing of cultural expressions and practices, forbidding the Kurdish language, and repressing civic and political organizations, eventually escalating to massive military assaults killing tens of thousands of Kurds and to the burning or bombing of villages into oblivion. The Western response to these atrocities has also followed a familiar pattern of diplomatic silence and overall indifference complemented by periodic alliances with Kurdish groups lacking any follow-through and ending with the branding of any armed Kurdish resistance as terrorism. The West has a vested interest in allowing this same process to continue, using the Kurds time and time again as a scapegoat in regional alliances and manipulations of an ever-expanding web of complexity.

In 1978, in a tea house in Istanbul, a new chapter in Kurdish resistance began with the founding of the Kurdistan Workers' Party (PKK). The PKK was the first militant Kurdish resistance group to espouse explicitly Marxist ideology. It called for a communist Kurdistan and was a reflection of Turkey's radical left student and worker uprisings that had started that year. Immediately after its founding, the PKK conducted a string of high-profile assassinations and bombings in southern Turkey along with a highly successful recruitment drive. Part of the secret to the PKK's success in recruiting was its charismatic leader, Abdullah Öcalan—also known as Apo—and the party's emphasis on recruiting not only men but women. In 1980, there was another Turkish military coup, aimed to restore order in the state. That year saw the arrest of some of the PKK top leadership and the exile of most of the central committee to Syria and Western

Europe. The Turkish military was able to thwart many PKK operations and put pressure on PKK strongholds and training bases in the southeast. The PKK found its ability to act inside Turkey limited and began its first bombing operations in Europe. The PKK also found partners in other radical Marxists groups like the Palestinian Liberation Organization (PLO), the Communist League of Iran, and the ASALA, a Marxist Armenian guerrilla group. These groups had more connections and better access to resources than the relatively new PKK did in exile.

With the PKK central committee scattered and its training bases and offices in Turkey shut down, a more decentralized structure began to appear. Training bases were setup and operations were conducted in a variety of European (Belgium and Germany) and Middle Eastern countries (notably Iraq and Syria). In 1984, after civilian rule was restored in Turkey and a number of political prisoners were released, the PKK was again able to rebuild its militant presence in Turkey. The PKK launched a full-scale guerrilla war, mostly in the south of Turkey bust occasionally reaching as far north as Istanbul. They employed a variety of tactics including kidnappings, industrial sabotage, assassinations of police and military officers, and bombings while also providing social services and cultural events for the repressed Kurdish communities in the south. The new Turkish civilian government responded with the collective punishments of entire villages, military occupation of the Kurdish regions, and a series of draconian laws targeted at the PKK and their alleged Kurdish supporters. Tens of thousands of people in Turkey, including a great many civilians (90% of them Kurdish), lost their lives in this conflict, which lasted until a ceasefire was declared in 2013.

Turkey has always considered the PKK a terrorist organization, making it official in 1979. NATO, of which Turkey has been a key member since 1952, was lobbied heavily by Turkey in the 1990s to add the PKK and its sister organizations to the official terrorist watch-list, and in 2003 NATO conceded. The year before, both the EU and the US both added the PKK to their terrorist lists, where they remain to this day. A number of Western countries with strong economic and political links to Turkey have used the "terrorist" designation to hound the PKK by seizing assets, deporting PKK supporters, shutting down satellite and radio stations sympathetic to the PKK, and providing billions in aid to Turkey for "its war on terrorism." Turkey has also used the PKK's terrorist label to avoid criticisms of human rights abuses and to ignore over a dozen international courts' rulings against their treatment of Kurds. Today Turkey has over a hundred Kurdish organizations on its terrorist list, yet it refuses to place ISIS on that same list. It is clear that Turkey is less interested in waging a war on terrorism than it is in waging a war against the Kurdish people.

The Islamic State of Iraq and al-Sham (ISIS) declared itself to be the only legitimate Islamic Caliphate in mid-2014, going so far as to rename itself simply the Islamic State (IS). ISIS has seized large swathes of territory across Eastern Syria and Western Iraq, and it is now the most well-funded and well-armed jihadist group in the world. ISIS operates with a daily hunger for atrocity previously unknown in the region, resurrecting practices of mass rape, sex slavery, and crucifixion, and it happily announces policies of ethnic cleansing and genocide. Turkey and other major regional powers have been wary of directly confronting ISIS, instead seeking to transform of the threat of such a group into political capital and concessions from world powers.

Despite its current meteoric rise, ISIS did not burst recently onto the scene in a simplistic blitzkrieg of hardline puritanical Sunni ideology—it has been building its forces since the American invasion of Iraq in 2003. Formerly an offshoot of Al-Qaeda in Iraq, ISIS gained valuable military experience fighting NATO forces in Fallujah during the initial years of the Coalition Occupation of Iraq, eventually rebranding itself the Islamic State of Iraq. Prophetic rebranding aside, the Islamic State of Iraq built its formidable force in Iraq during the mid and late 2000s before shifting focus to the growing unrest and chaos of the Syrian civil war. ISIS considers practitioners of anything besides their own brand of Sunni Islam to be infidels deserving death, and takes special pleasure in annihilating Shia Muslims and minorities such as the Yazidis and the Kurds—both of whom would be among the few groups to stand up to their orgy of violence and slaughter.

The Great Game: World Powers and the Kurds

The Kurdish Question has never been a strictly regional affair. Since before World War I until today, powers stretched over the entire globe—from Australia to America—have been involved in this issue. From Iraq to Egypt, the Kurds have been used as pawns to leverage the players of the region. Just like in a game of chess, the Kurdish pawn is often sacrificed to gain a better position on the board. Over and over again, foreign powers intervene for a brief period of time, encouraging Kurdish rebellion just to withdraw support at crucial points and sacrificing the Kurds when they are no longer needed. Sometimes world powers support one Kurdish rebellion while simultaneously backing another regime's crackdown on Kurdish villages only a few hundred miles away across the border. Kurdish autonomy has been used as a functional and disposable tool for achieving other countries' agendas from the realignment of the region after WWI, the rise of Soviet power, through the Cold War and the spread of Nasserism, to George Bush Sr.'s New World Order. Kurdish autonomy has always been a means to end, never an end to itself, for the many states that have gotten involved over the years. Owing to their precarious position, the Kurds have been led to naively believe, decade after decade, that the world powers actually cared about their cause while they were being manipulated for someone else's momentary geopolitical advantage.

The Soviet Union's relationship to both its own 450,000 Kurds and the Kurds in Kurdistan was also marked mostly by state suspicion and repression. In the first years of the Soviet Union, Kurds, like many other minority groups, were forcibly displaced and a special regional government unit was set up to monitor them. This regional unit was reorganized several times and ultimately disbanded in 1930 when the Stalinist central government feared it had become too sympathetic to the Kurds. Under Stalin, tens of thousands of Kurds were deported from Azerbaijan and Armenia to Kazakhstan, while Kurds in Georgia became victims of the purges that followed the end of WWII. Through the 1960s, various measures were taken by the Soviet

Regime to marginalize and oppress its Kurdish population. In the 1980s the PKK, the only Kurdish political party to partner with Kurds in the USSR, began collaboration with Kurds living in the Transcaucasia region and made serious inroads with the population there. By 1986, non-armed PKK support organizations had formed in the USSR, though they were technically illegal. According to Turkish press, there was even a PKK organization in Kazakhstan in 2004.

For the most part the Soviet Union, and later the Russian Federation, has not been involved directly with Kurdish Independence since the 1940s, when it supported an autonomous Kurdish state in Iran. Despite the PKK's early communist roots, the Soviet Union never supported it because of the USSR's ties with Syria and Turkey. Today the Russian Federation is reluctant to actively support Kurdish independence in Kurdistan because of its own restive minorities, including the Russian Kurds. At various times the PKK has sought support for training bases, weapons, resources, and a place for exiles from other communist regimes, including Cuba, Angola, Vietnam and others, but not a one of those countries was interested in supporting their communist cousins in such a complicated geopolitical area without backing from the USSR. Some socialist countries did bring up UN resolutions, and most of the Soviet sphere voted for measures in support of Kurdish autonomy in Kurdistan. Russia, along with UN Security Council member China, has also refused to designate the PKK or any other Kurdish political groups as terrorist organizations.

Western governments and organizations such as NATO have been involved in one side or another of the Kurdish questions since the early 19th century at the dawn of the Kurdish autonomy movement. The French and the British foreign offices have used various regional Kurds and their dreams of autonomy as proxies to secure their mandates in the Middle East and to thwart each other. During particular crises, for example immediately following World War I and World War II, shadowy diplomats were shuttling between Paris or London to Kurdish shepherd villages, bringing a little aid and vague promises of support if the Kurds supported their particular political machinations. European powers did not limit their role to just the territory of Kurdistan either, and also used their home countries to get involved in the Kurdish Question. Countries like Germany, Belgium, and the Netherlands for a while allowed militant Kurdish training bases to operate on their soil but would raid and shut them down depending on the geopolitical winds of the time. Greece supplied Kurds in Turkey and housed exiled PKK officials in order to punish Turkey for their 1974 invasion of Cyprus, but after coming to agreement on trade with Turkey they kicked the PKK out and stopped all aid. France even tried to use Kurds to slow Algerian independence, despite the fact that there were no Kurds in Algeria, by implying they may give them territory in a French-owned Algeria.

The US was late to the show of manipulating the Kurds' desire for freedom. During the Cold War the US mostly found itself siding with the Shah of Iran and using CIA personnel and resources to help both repress the Kurds in Iran and foment Kurdish rebellions in Iraq. The US stuck to covert operations, and thus little was known until recently about US involvement in the Kurdish Question. During the first Gulf War, when Iraq occupied the oil-rich emirate of Kuwait in August 1990, Saddam Hussein became America's enemy number one. Yet from

1987 until the Iraqi invasion of Kuwait, the US said nothing. At times, the US even supported Iraq in the UN, when Saddam Hussein was gassing tens of thousands of Kurds and bombing whole Kurdish towns and villages. But at the beginning of the First Gulf War, George Bush Sr. publicly declared Kurds are the US's "natural allies" and suggested they should revolt against the Baghdad regime. Of course, Bush Sr. knew that the Kurds had already been fighting the Ba'athist regime in a bloody, fifteen-year, on-again off-again civil war.

After the war, the US put in place an ineffective no fly zone, which apparently did not include helicopters, to "protect the Kurds/" Thousands of Kurds and other civilians in northern Iraq were killed by Saddam's military while US planes flew overhead doing nothing. During the second Gulf War, the US asked again for the peshmerga (the military forces of Iraqi Kurdistan) to help rid the country of the Ba'athist regime. This time, the Kurds decided to focus on securing the north for themselves and on creating an army that could defend itself—they'd learned their lesson from the first Gulf War. Today the Kurdistan Regional Government (KRG) exists not because the US protected the Kurds, but because they took US and coalition aid and resources to prepare their own defense. The KRG also pursued its own diplomatic strategy with the fledgling and factious National Iraqi Congress.

Many other countries, from China to Australia, have interfered in the Kurdish Question, ultimately thwarting the Kurdish dream of freedom across a unified Kurdistan. Today almost all countries in the West have designated Kurdish militant groups as terrorists while at the same time trying to enlist their help in the war against the Islamic State and other Jihadist groups. It seems the Kurds have lost some of their naivete and have learned that being temporary sacrificial pawns for the West will not aid their cause in the long run. The lesson of the second Gulf War and the recent Syrian civil war is that the Kurds must rely on their own forces to have any hope of securing autonomy and justice for their people.

From Red Star to Ishtar's Star

While the PKK was not founded by die-hard communists, it soon became a classic Maoist national liberation struggle party complete with an unquestioned charismatic "father of the people", Abdullah Öcalan, a.k.a Apo. There was little to differentiate the PKK from the dozens of Mao-inspired militant liberation groups of the late 1970s and 1980s.

The PKK weren't the only committed Marxists in Kurdistan— a number of other smaller groups existed, some claiming to be Leninists, Trotskyites, or even Titoists. But the peasant-based insurrectionary philosophy of Maoism, as espoused by the polit-bureau and the leadership of the PKK, was by far the most popular and militarily effective means of resisting oppression.

The PKK's flamboyant embrace of communism garnered some support from the calcified old Left parties of Western Europe, but it failed to produce much in the way of real solidarity. While certain Maoist ideas appealed to Kurds eager to rid themselves of authoritarian state repression, those same ideas alienated a lot of potential, more liberal, supporters. Thus, the PKK's struggles were largely ignored and sometimes condemned by possible sympathizers in and outside the region. The emphasis on centralization in Maoist communism also alienated many of the social leaders inside Kurdistan. The Kurds traditionally have been socially and politically organized by loosely connected tribes and have supported tribal leaders who had distinguished themselves in some way other than heredity. Periodically, Kurds formed large, temporary confederations of tribes to mount uprisings and military actions. Political parties have never gained the monopoly on political organizing that they have in many other parts of the world—it wasn't uncommon for a Kurd to be part of a few political parties and switch between them based on how successful they were. Despite these cultural obstacles, the PKK championed hardline communism until well after the fall of the Soviet regime.

For the PKK, the crisis in their communist faith didn't occur until 1999 when their leader Öcalan was arrested in Nairobi by the MIT (Turkish military intelligence), flown back to Turkey, and incarcerated on a prison island upon which he was the only inmate. The Turkish media showed a humiliated Öcalan, "the Terrorist of Turkey," harmless and in chains. With their leader captured and no obvious successor, the PKK's central committee was thrown into crisis. The increasingly militant tactics of bombings, roadside ambushes, and suicide bombers were not working, and the rise of Jihadi attacks in the Middle East and the West made the PKK seem just like another Islamic terrorist organization despite its communist ideology. This combined, with the collapse of communism in Eastern Europe and Russia, led to a period of ideological soul-searching for the PKK and its leader.

Thousands of miles away, on January 1, 1994 (five years before Öcalan's capture) a new type of liberation struggle kicked off in the forgotten mountain jungles of Chiapas, Mexico. The Zapatistas, with their red star flag and their black masks, burst onto the world stage and quickly inspired the progressive Left around the world. A small Mayan liberation struggle had risen from the Lacandon Jungle of Southern Mexico and declared themselves autonomous. These politically savvy revolutionaries created a new type of leftist insurrectionary political configuration they called Zapatismo. Zapatismo situated itself as a mode of liberation and leftist struggle that rejected hierarchy, party control, and aspirations to create a State apparatus. The architects of this new configuration had spent years in hardline Marxist guerrilla organizations in Mexico before rejecting that model of struggle and seeking a new approach.

Öcalan and the other leaders in the central committee of the PKK were familiar with the rapid rise and success of the Zapatistas. A year before his arrest, Öcalan had spoken to PKK party leaders about Zapatismo at a two-day conference. And in his first months of imprisonment, Apo had a "crisis of faith" regarding doctrinaire Marxist ideology and its ability to free the Kurds. Öcalan, who spent much of his life espousing a hardline Stalinist doctrine, started to reject Marxism-Leninism in favor of direct democracy. He had concluded that Marxism was authoritarian, dogmatic, and unable to creatively reflect the real problems facing the Kurdish resistance. In prison, Apo started reading anarchist and post-Marxist works including Emma Goldman, Foucalt, Wallerstein, Braudel, and Murray Bookchin. Öcalan was particularly impressed with Bookchin's anarchist philosophy of ecological municipalism, going so far as to demand that all PKK leaders read Bookchin. From inside prison, Öcalan absorbed Bookchin's ideas (most notably Bookchin's, *Civilization Narratives*) and wrote his own book based on these ideas, *The Roots of Civilization* (2001). It was Bookchin's, *Ecology of Freedom* (1985), however, which Öcalan made required reading for all PKK militants. It went on to influence the ideas found in Rojava.

In 2004, Öcalan tried to arrange a meeting with Bookchin through his lawyers, describing himself as Bookchin's "student" and eager to adapt Bookchin's ideas to the Kurdish question. In particular, Öcalan wanted to discuss his newest manuscript, *In Defense of People* (2004), which he had hoped would change the discourse of the Kurdish struggle. Unfortunately for Öcalan, the 83-year-old Bookchin was too ill to accept the request and sent back a message of support instead. Murray Bookchin died of congested heart failure two years later, in 2006. A PKK congress held later that year hailed the American thinker as "one of the greatest social scientists of the 20th century," and vowed that "Bookchin's thesis on the state, power, and hierarchy will be implemented and realized through our struggle.... We will put this promise into practice, this as the first society that establishes a tangible democratic confederalism." Five years later, in 2011, the Syrian civil war gave the Kurds a chance to try to make good on their promise.

The Syrian civil war began as part of the general uprisings in spring 2011 in North Africa and the Middle East that the West dubbed the "Arab Spring." Kurds from a variety of political backgrounds joined students, Islamists, workers, political dissents, and others in calling for the end of the repression of the Assad dictatorship. Syrian President Bashar al-Assad, however, had learned the lessons of Tunisia, Libya, and Egypt and quickly sent in troops to crush the growing democratic movement. By autumn, the mostly peaceful protests that had taken place in the spring had morphed into a full-on armed insurrection against the Assad regime.

When the protests first began, Assad's government finally granted citizenship to an estimated 200,000 stateless Kurds in an effort to neutralize potential Kurdish opposition. By the beginning of 2012, when over 50% of the country was controlled by rebel groups and Islamic militias, and Assad's forces were spread thin, the regime decided to pull all military and government officials out of the Kurdish regions in the north, in effect handing the region over to the Kurds and Yezedis living there. Opposition groups, most prominently the PKK-aligned Democratic Union Party (PYD), created a number of coalition superstructures to administer the region. There was tension between PYD and parties aligned with the in Iraq (KRG), however, and at one time there were even two competing coalitions: the PYD-backed National Coordination Committee for Democratic Change (NCC) and the KRG-aligned Kurdish National Council (KNC). In early 2012, when it looked like the tension between the two groups might result in armed conflict, the President of the KRG Massoud Barzani and leaders of the PKK brought the two groups together to form a new coalition called the Supreme Kurdish Council (SKC) made up of over fifteen political parties and hundreds of community councils. Within months of forming, the SKC changed its name to the Democratic Society Movement (TEV-DEM) and added non-Kurdish groups, political parties, and organizations to the coalition. The TEV-DEM created an interim governing body for the Rojava region.

The TEV-DEM's program was heavily influenced by the PYD's ideas of "democratic confederalism," which the PKK had adopted as their official platform in a people's congress on May 17th, 2005. According to the platform, and subsequent documents and proclamations from Rojava, "democratic confederalism of Rojava is not a State system, it is the democratic system of a people without a State... It takes its power from the people and adopts to reach self-sufficiency in every field, including economy." In Rojava, Democratic Confederalist ideology has three main planks: libertarian municipalism, radical pluralism, and social ecology. The TEV-DEM have been implementing this new social vision on a massive scale in Rojava since early 2012. The PKK has attempted (and succeeded to some degree) to implement democratic confederalism in scattered villages in Turkey along the Iraq border since 2009, experiments that served as an inspiration for much of the Rojava revolution. This vision, in both Turkey and in Rojava, draws heavily from contemporary anarchist, feminist, and ecological thought.

Stateless Government: Radical Democracy and Decentralization

How do you base a government on anarchism? Rojava is not the first, and hopefully won't be the last, experiment in creating a new form of a decentralized non-state government without hierarchy. In the past two years, two-and-half million people in Rojava have been participating in this new form of governance, a governance related to that of the Spanish Revolution

(1936), the Zapatistas (1994), the Argentinian Neighborhood Assembly Movement (2001-2003), and Murray Bookchin's libertarian municipalism. Despite some similarities to these past experiments and ideas, what is being implemented in war-torn Rojava is unique—and it's extremely ambitious. It's no hyperbole to say that this revolution in northern Syria is historic, especially for anarchists.

At the core of this social experiment are the variety of "local councils" that encourage maximum participation by the people of Rojava. The Kurdish people have a long history of local assemblies based on tribal and familial allegiances. These semi-formal assemblies have been an important practice of social organizing for Kurds for hundreds of years, so it is no surprise that the face-to-face assemblies soon became the backbone of their new government. In Rojava, neighborhood assemblies make up the largest number of councils. Every person (including teenagers) can participate in an assembly near where they live. In addition to these neighborhood assemblies, there are councils based on workplaces, civic organizations, religious organizations, political parties, and other affinity-based councils (e.g. Youth). People often are part of a number of local councils depending on their life circumstances. These councils can be as small as a couple dozen people or they can have hundreds of participants. But regardless of size, they operate similarly. The councils work on a direct democracy model, meaning that anyone at the council may speak, suggest topics to be decided upon, and vote on proposals (though many councils use consensus for their decision-making). It is unclear how membership is determined in these councils, but we know that the opposition movement councils prior to 2012 had no fixed membership and anyone showing up at assembly could fully participate. It is also unclear how often these councils meet and who determines when they meet. It is known that the neighborhood assemblies in the Efrin Canton meet weekly, as does one of the hospital workers' councils. These local councils make up the indivisible unit of Rojava democracy. Larger bodies (e.g. Supreme Council of the Rojava cantons) are populated with representatives from these local councils. All decisions from these "upper councils" must be formally adopted by the local councils to be binding for their constituents. This is very different from the federalist tradition, in which the federation supersedes local control. In August 2014, for example, a regional council decided that local security forces could carry weapons while patrolling a city, but three local assemblies did not approve this decision, so in those local assembly areas security must refrain from carrying weapons. The role of the "upper councils" is currently limited to coordination between the myriad of local councils while all power is still held locally. Representatives to the "upper councils" rotate frequently, with a maximum term set by the "upper council," but local councils often create their own guidelines for more frequent rotation of their representatives. The goal of the Rojava council system is to maximize local power and to decentralize while achieving a certain necessary degree of regional coordination and information-sharing.

The remaining government above the upper council level seems similar to a council parliamentary system with rotating representatives, an executive branch composed of canton co-presidents, and an independent judiciary. All governmental power emanates from the councils, and the councils retain local autonomy, thus forming a confederation. The confederation is made up of three autonomous cantons that have their own ministries and militias. There is no federal government in the Rojava canton system. Voluntary association and mutual aid are key concepts for the confederation, as these ideas protect local autonomy. Voluntary association leads to radical decentralization, severely limiting any organizational structures above the primary decision-makers of the local councils. All bodies beyond the local councils must have proportional representation of the ethnic communities in the canton and at least 40% gender balance (this includes all ministries). Most ministries have co-ministers with one male and one female minister, with the exception of the Women's Minister. Most decisions by the Supreme Council need support of 2/3 of the delegates from the upper councils. Any canton retains autonomy from Supreme Council decisions and may override them in their own People's Assembly (the largest upper council of any region) while still being part of the confederation. This bottom-up decentralization seeks to preserve the maximum level of autonomy for local people while encouraging maximum political participation.

Both internal and external security for the cantons is administered by each canton's People's Assembly. The local security, which are equivalent to police, are called Asayish (security in Kurdish). The Asayish are elected by local councils and serve a specific term determined by the local council and the canton's People's Assembly. The Asayish have also their own assembly (but not one that can send representatives to the People's Assembly), in which they elect officers and make other decisions. In addition to the Asayish, there are people's self-defense militias to provide security from outside threats (e.g. currently the

Islamic State, but this could also include regional and state government forces). These militias elect their own officers but are directly responsible to the canton's People's Assembly. Both the Asayish and the people's self-defense militias have two organizations: one a female-only group and the other co-ed. Militias that are providing mutual aid in another canton (Asayish are for the most part forbidden to work in other cantons) must follow that canton's People's Assembly but can retain their own commanders and units. In times of peace, the cantons do not maintain standing militia service.

Rojava's relationship with the Syrian state is yet to be tested. The Rojava Canton Confederation is not set up as a state. It draws instead on the idea of dual power, an idea first outlined by the French anarchist Proudhon. The KCC described dual power as "a strategy of achieving a libertarian socialist economy and political and social autonomy by means of incrementally establishing and then networking institutions of direct participatory democracy" to contest the existing authority of state-capitalism. Rojava currently has set out a path of co-existence with whatever state arises from the Syrian civil war and to the current alignment of neighboring states (namely Turkey, Iraq, and Iran) that encompass Kurdistan. People in Rojava would maintain their Syrian citizenship and participate in the Syrian state so long as it doesn't directly contradict the Rojava principles. This uneasy co-existence is the reason the cantons have explicitly forbidden national flags, have not created a new currency, a foreign ministry, or national passports and identity papers, and why they do not have a standing army. It is unclear if the people of Rojava plan to maintain this relationship with the state or what would happen in conflictual situations.

Rojava is neither a state nor a pure anarchist society. It is an ambitious social experiment that has rejected the seduction of state power and nationalism and has instead embraced autonomy, direct democracy, and decentralization to create a freer society for people in Rojava. The Rojava principles have borrowed from anarchism, social ecology, and feminism in an attempt to chart a societal vision that emphasizes accountability and independence for a radically pluralistic community. It is unclear whether this experiment will move towards greater decentralization of the kind Bookchin suggests and the Zapatistas have implemented or if it will become more centralized and federal as, happened after both the Russian and Spanish revolutions. What is happening right now is a historic departure from traditional national-liberation struggle and should be of great interest to anti-authoritarians everywhere.

Radical Pluralism

While we see the Rojava revolution as a Kurdish movement, we should not overlook the dynamic pluralism of the region and the aspirations of the peoples of the three cantons that make of the Rojava Confederation. We should also take into account the fact that the Kurds themselves are not a homogenous people, but instead one made up of numerous distinct tribal groups and four religions. The Kurdish diaspora had found numerous Kurds, including many of the Kurd's ideological leaders, living in cities and attending universities across Europe. This culture exposure helped instill a tolerant and pluralistic outlook in

Kurdistan. The Rojava Principles not only talk about pluralism and diversity in regards to ethnicity and faith, but have created organizing structures to maximize these principles in practice.

The Rojava region is dominated by Kurds, with around 65% of the population identifying as Kurdish. The remaining 35% is made up of Arabs, Armenians, and Assyrians. There has been immigration of both Kurds and non-Kurds to the region from war-torn areas of Syria. It is estimated (though the numbers are very unreliable) that over 200,000 people have relocated to Rojava since the beginning of the war from other parts of Syria. A substantial number of these new immigrants belong to religious and ethnic minorities from Syria and Eastern Iraq.

As regards religion, the Kurds are the most diverse ethnicity in the region. The majority of Kurds (55-65%) are Sunni Muslims, belonging to the Shafi sect. There are also Muslim Kurds who follow Shia, Sufi, and Alawi traditions. There is a sizable number of Christian Kurds, many of whom immigrated to Rojava after the start of the war. Yazidis have also immigrated to Rojava. Yazidis are a syncretic religion that has connections to Zoroastrianism, Judaism, and Islam. A small minority in Rojava follows a new form of Zoroastrianism, and there is also a very small pocket of Kurdish Jews. Most of these religious groups traditionally lived in communities side-by-side, partially due to forced resettlements and self-exiles, and many even shared religious buildings. There is a also a high percentage of inter-faith marriages.

Rojava has embraced its diversity and is explicit about its commitment to pluralism. They use the term radical pluralism to describe how their approach differs from the extreme sectarianism found in much of the region. There are specific local councils for each ethnic group and religious organization. In, addition upper councils (e.g. City and Regional Councils) have ethnic quotas to ensure that all ethnic groups are represented. A similar quota system exists in all ministries except the specific ethnic and religious ministries. The Rojava Principles also enshrine a number of protections for ethnic and religious minorities (including those without any faith). Even militias and security have explicit pluralistic characteristics with different ethnic and religious groups working together.

Rojava has staked out a new path of pluralism that doesn't currently exist anywhere else in the region. Rojava has rejected the call of secularism, like that of Turkey, that oppresses religious organizations and practitioners in exchange for a pluralistic society, but instead has set itself as a safe haven of respect and political empowerment for ethnic minorities in the region.

Feminism in the Rojava Republics

Kurdish female fighters have recently been "discovered" and sensationalized by Western media—even fashion magazines have entered the fray. But this media is simply glamorizing female fighters without paying but little attention to their politics. It is all too easy to fall into the media trap of fetishizing the female fighters of the all-women Women's Self-Defense Brigades (the YPJ) and the mixed-gender General Self-Defense Brigades (the YPG) in Kurdistan without considering the implications of women choosing to be fighters in a very patriarchal society. The women who are fighting in Rojava are fighting for their lives and they are fighting for their rights as women against an enemy that rapes and sells women as sex slaves. But this isn't a new thing—women who have been fighting in the region for decades. In fact, traditionally, half the members of the PKK have been women. What *is* new about the women combatants of Rojava is their explicit feminism, a feminism that has become one of the founding principles of the Rojava experiment. Kurdish culture is generally strongly patriarchal: male dominance is prevalent, and arranged and forced marriages are common. The YPJ are not only fighting against ISIS, they are fighting for feminism and gender equality—and they're doing it with ideas and bullets alike.

The YPJ exists as a counterpoint to the YPG. Women of Rojava hope that at some point the YPJ will no longer be necessary, but until that point it will function as an entirely-female force for both fighting Rojava's enemies and resolving social issues. The YPJ is meant to eventually become part of the YPG, but in a show of idealistic pragmatism, the KCK has designated that at least for the foreseeable future the YPJ as an exclusively female fighting force will be needed to balance out the traditionally masculine-oriented militarism of armed militias such as the YPG (or its parent organization, the PYD). Furthermore, while the leadership of all governing councils of the Rojava cantons are mandated to be composed of at least 40% of either gender, the leadership of the YPG is often more like 50-60% women as it recruits heavily from the leadership of the YPJ. In addition to the YPJ militia, the all-female security force Asayish-J (*Asayish* being the Kurdish for "Security") is alone responsible for crimes involving women, children, domestic abuse, and hate crimes, while also independently operating checkpoints and conducting other functions of the "standard" Asayish.

Of course, the YPJ calls to mind other all-female fighting forces—perhaps most famously, the *Mujeres Libres* of the Spanish civil war. This parallel is both accurate and dangerous, as the Mujeres Libres did indeed form a fearsome fighting force for the inherently radical political notion of sexual and gender equality, but unfortunately they've also become an idea that many radicals have placed on a pedestal and exalted without seeing the Free Women of Spain as human. We must not compound that same mistake with Orientalism when it comes to feminism in Rojava; these are real people risking their lives for powerful political ideas. They're not the storybook women the media caricatured by popular media as "badass," "sexy amazons" because they have taken up arms.

One of the other ways the Rojavans have been fighting for the rights of women in Kurdistan has been the creation of all-women's houses run by the Asayish-J. These are houses where any woman over the age of 15 can go and stay for as long as they'd like and receive free education, and then return home (if they so chose) whenever they'd like. No men are allowed in these houses, so as to protect the houses' integrity and to ensure that the women feel comfortable and secure. There are currently 30 of these centers across Rojava. And as a response to suicides caused by forced marriage, the Asayish-J runs a hotline for women which offers emotional and physical support at any time.

Feminism in Rojava transcends just the YPJ and the Asayish-J and is one of the three founding principles of the Rojavan Revolution. Society, as envisioned in the Rojava Principles, must be set on a new path towards feminism and simply declaring support for feminism is not enough. With this in mind, feminism is an essential practice of all social interactions in the three cantons, and women are considered true political actors with genuine agency—which is revolutionary in and of itself.

A People's Economy

The Rojava revolution's economic plan is called a "People's Economy" to differentiate it from traditional market and socialist (i.e. state) economies. But though it posits itself as an alternative to the dualism of capitalism and communism, it is really not a fully formed model as of yet. There are three major concepts in the People's Economy: commons, private property based on use, and worker-administered businesses. The Rojava economic experiment is less an implementation of a single concept than a jury-rigged system that must respond to the needs of a war and a crippling economic embargo.

In 2010, a year before the Arab Spring exploded in Syria, the Rojava region provided over 40% of the country's GNP and 70% of its exports despite only about 17% of Syria's population living in the region. And yet people in Rojava made well below the median income of the country. The Rojava region sits on the famous Mesopotamian Plain, between the Euphrates and Tigris rivers, and is the oldest agricultural center in the world. Until 2011, northern Syria exported grain, cotton, and meat to its neighbors and Europe and was the country's largest producer of oil. Plentiful water from the region's rivers allowed for cement factories and other medium industrial plants to be built in the area in the 1970s and 1980s. However, since the start of the Syrian civil war, the infrastructure required to support these economic activities has been falling apart. Power, communications, roads, and railways have all been seriously compromised. Failed infrastructure, constant war, and a strictly-enforced embargo (most notably by Turkey, which shares Rojava's only stable border), have ruined the traditional economy of the area. In 2012, the PYD launched what it originally called the Social Economy Plan, which would later be renamed the People's Economy Plan (PEP). The PEP was based on the writings of Öcalan and the lived experiences of Kurds in North Kurdistan (southern Turkey).

Traditional "private property" was abolished in late 2012, meaning all buildings, land, and infrastructure fell under control of the various city councils. This did not mean people no longer owned their homes or businesses, however. The councils implemented an "ownership by use" sovereign principle, a principle that could not be overturned by any council. Ownership by use means that when a building like a home or a business is being used by a person or persons, the users would in fact own the land and structures but would not be able to sell them on an open market. Öcalan wrote that use ownership is what prevents speculation and capital accumulation which in turn leads to exploitation. Aside from property owned by use, in principle any other property would become commons. This abolishing of private property did not extend to commodities like automobiles, machines, electronics, furniture, etc. but was limited to land, infrastructure, and structures.

The commons encompasses land, infrastructure, and buildings not owned by individuals but held in stewardship by the councils. Councils can turn over these public goods to individuals to be used. Commons are conceived of as a way to provide both a safety net for those without resources and a way to maximize use of the material resources of the community. Commons also include the ecological aspects of the region including water, parks, wildlife and wilderness, and even most livestock. According to Dr. Ahmad Yousef, an economic co-minister, three-quarters of traditional private property is being used as commons and one quarter is still being owned by use of individuals. The economic plan (PEP) posits that the commons are robust enough economically that there is no need for taxes, and since the beginning of the Rojava revolution there have been no taxes of any type.

Worker administration is the third leg of the stool of the economic plan. Workers are to control the means of production in their workplace through worker councils that are responsible to the local councils. According to the Ministry of Economics, worker councils have only been set up for about one third of the enterprises in Rojava so far. Worker councils are coordinated by the various economic ministries and local councils to assure a smooth flow of goods, supplies, and other essentials.

The PEP also calls for all economic activity in the cantons to be ecologically sound. It is unclear who has responsibility for this, whether it is the workers' councils, the local councils, the City Councils, or the Peoples' assemblies. Throughout the various statements from the economic ministries, one sees mention over and over again about the primacy of ecologically sensible industry—but details are lacking.

The PEP is also vague when it comes to its relationship with other economies inside and outside of Syria. A substantial amount of the current economic activity in the region comes from black market oil being sold outside the region. In Autumn, 2014, representatives of Rojava travelled around Europe looking to create "trading partners" and seemed to be suggesting a standard free market policy, while at the same time eliminating banks and other financial institutions inside Rojava. The Rojava canton principles also clearly state that the region will not produce its own money or bonds, so it is unclear how such trading relationships between other governments would actually come to pass even if the embargo is lifted.

The strength of the PEP seems to be in how it humanizes economics for local people. It achieves this by both having commons available to the community to provide for those in need and by creating small-scale limited ownership to promote and meet local needs and markets. Worker administration increases and expands participation in the local economy and makes the economy more accountable to those directly affected by it. The PEP seeks to create a self-sufficiency that is aligned with ecological stewardship that actually puts people and the planet before profits. In short, the PEP is trying to create localized participatory economics to match the localized participatory governance.

Rojava Can't Wait and Neither Can We

Radicals in the West have been mostly silent as regards the Rojava Revolution, and we find ourselves in a strange situation where the mainstream media seems more interested in these events than we are. There are of course a number of reasons, and excuses, for this lack of interest in the revolutionary experiment going on in Northern Syria.

The most commonly voiced objection on the Left to supporting the Rojava revolution is that its motives are unclear or suspect. Anarchists have a long history of seeing popular revolutions in other places being neutered by liberal elements or even hijacked by Leftist authoritarian groups. Many on the Left are concerned by the role the PKK and its proxies play in this revolution. The PKK had a thirty-year history of unwavering support for a Stalinist/Maoist ideology and practice that has rightfully alienated much of the libertarian Left in the West. In particular, the PKK's hardline authoritarianism and their sectarian tendency to violently silence any dissent among radicals in Kurdistan has rightfully seen support for the PKK dry up in Europe and in North America. But for more than a decade now, since Öcalan has been jailed, the PKK has been claiming a more anarchistic organizing model and have since worked with a number of other radical groups. More importantly, Rojava, which has a strong PKK proxy presence through the PYD, has not only rejected authoritarianism in words and writings but more obviously in practice. Even if one remains skeptical of the PKK and PYD, the fact that currently there is nothing authoritarian or sectarian in the political structures of Rojava should give the West some cause to hold their skepticism.

Whether this is because the PKK has changed of its own volition or because it was forced to change by the people doesn't really matter. The only question in this regard is how is the revolution is being manifested in words and actions, and whether these actions and words are authoritarian or sectarian. Any sincere analysis of the past two years in Rojava shows an honest commitment to pluralistic and decentralized ideas, words, and practice. The PKK's sketchy past makes it that more incumbent on Western revolutionaries and anarchists to support the Rojava revolution now. If the PKK has *not* really changed, then we need to support and buttress where we can the ideology of anti-authoritarianism and radical decentralization to avoid any compromise of the current revolution by the PKK or any other authoritarians of the left. And if the PKK *has* changed, then all the more reason to support a political project that is authentically radical and liberatory.

Many of us are rightfully confused by the complexities of the Kurdish struggle and the politics of the region. This is understandable, but complexity should not be an excuse for us withholding solidarity and support. Every day there are new resources (including this small book) that explain the complex history not only of the long Kurdish struggle but also that of the entire region. We can learn about it. This has been done before. For instance, the Palestinian struggle is also extremely complex and nuanced but the radical left has taken it upon itself to make the struggle understandable. We must educate ourselves and others on the Kurdish struggle and that in Rojava in particular instead of withdrawing from this historic situation or waiting for others, who do not share our politics or the politics of the Rojava revolution, to explain it to us.

There are many radicals suspicious of the Kurds, and by extension of Rojava, because of the US government's military support of the YPG/YPJ fighters. The US has used Kurdish fighters as proxies for the past twenty years in various conflicts in the Middle East. There is a concern that Rojava is or will become a puppet state of US interests in the region, something most US radicals would not be willing to support. But support for the anti-capitalist and anti-state revolution in Rojava can hardly be seen as implicit support for US political interests abroad. It seems clear that the US' current support of Rojava is simply a matter of pragmatism to further their attempt to "degrade" ISIS. The Rojava revolution is not specifically anti-American, but it *is* explicitly anti-capitalist and anti-state, which is something we can and should fully support. To ignore these facts is to play the same essentialist game that so often constricts Western radicals to fields of academia and theory.

The geographical distance and isolation, along with a lack of any sizable Kurdish immigrant population in the US, has made face-to-face connections difficult, thus forcing most people to rely on mainstream media for information about the region. While it is absolutely true that it is easier for radicals to travel to Chiapas, Greece, Palestine, or Ferguson than to northern Syria, we should not let that postpone our support and solidarity. Other means of communications have also been compromised because of the Syrian Government and the civil war. During the Arab spring the Syrian government severely limited the internet, going so far as to actually cut cable lines, and the civil war has since made internet extremely precarious in the region. The embargo and the closing of the Turkish/Syrian border by the Turkish military has also severely limited both travel and the flow of information. This geographic and informational isolation has undoubtedly retarded some support from the West's radical communities. But Mexico, the United States, and Israel have all tried some versions of these reprehensible tactics before, in their attempts to suppress support for other struggles, and that didn't stop us then. And if the danger is greater in Rojava, then so too is the necessity of our support. Every week activists in Rojava and elsewhere are opening up channels of communications that we should be actively engaged in.

There are numerous excuses for why radicals in the US might wish to wait to support the revolution in Rojava, but we can't afford to wait. While it is obvious the brave revolutionaries of Rojava could use our support now, we also need the Rojava revolution for our own work here in the West. Revolutionary politics in the West have been waiting far too long for an infusion of new ideas and practices, and the Rojavan Revolution in all of its facets is something we should support if we take our own politics at all seriously. The people of Rojava cannot wait for our support, and so too can we not wait for the selective safety of hindsight to analyze the revolution now unfolding. The people of Rojava have chosen to fight, and so must we.

A Kurdish YPJ fighter in Kobanê wrote to her mother:

I am fine mum. Yesterday we celebrated my 19th birthday.

My friend Azad sang a beautiful song about mothers. I remembered you and cried. Azad has a beautiful voice, he cried too when he was singing. He also missed his mother whom he has not seen for a year.

Yesterday we helped a wounded friend. He got wounded by two bullets. He didn't know much about the second wound when he was pointing to the first bullet in his chest. He was bleeding from his flank too, we bandaged his wound and I gave him my blood.

We are in the east side of Kobanî, mother.... A few miles only stand between us and them. We see their black flags, we listen to their radios, sometimes we don't understand what they say when they speak foreign languages but we can tell they are scared.

We are in a group of nine fighters. The youngest, Resho from Afrin. He fought in Tal Abyad then joined us. Alan is from

Qamishlo, from their best neighborhood, he fought in Sere Kaniye then joined us. He has a few scars on his body. He tells us it is for Avin. The oldest is Dersim, he is from the Qandil Mountain, and his wife was martyred in Diyarbekir and left him with two kids.

We are in a house on the outskirts of Kobani. We don't know much about its owners. There are photos of an old man and one of a young man with a black ribbon, seems like he is a martyr... There is a photo of Qazi Mohamad, Mulla Mustafa Barzani, Apo, and an old Ottoman map mentioning the name of Kurdistan.

We have not got coffee for a while, we found out that life is beautiful even without coffee. Honestly I've never had a coffee as good as yours mom.

We are here to defend a peaceful city. We never took part in killing anyone, instead we hosted many wounded and refugees from our Syrian brothers. We are defending a Muslim city that has tens of mosques. We are defending it from the barbaric forces.

Mother, I will visit you once this dirty war that was forced on us is over. I will be there with my friend Dersim who will go to Diyarbekir to meet his kids. We all miss home and want to go back to it, but this war does not know what missing means. Maybe I won't come back mother. Then be sure that I dreamed of seeing you for so long but I was not lucky.

I know that you will visit Kobanî one day and look for the house that witnessed my last days…it is on the east side of Kobanî. Part of it damaged, it has a green door which has many holes from sniper shots and you will see 3 windows, one on the east side, you will see my name written there in red ink…. Behind that window mother I waited counting my last moments watching the sunlight as it penetrated my room from the bullet holes in that window..

Behind that window, Azad sang his last song about his mother, he had a beautiful voice when he was saying "mum I miss you."

MuM I MISS YOU
Your daughter, Narin

The following is a statement and call for solidarity that was released online by "feminists and LGBTs of Turkey" in October, 2014.

A Call to Our Sisters and Comrades

WOMEN OF ROJAVA AND KURDISH WOMEN FIGHTERS HAVE made a revolution for an alternative life possible by sinking their teeth into it. It is an alternative life not only for women but also for all minorities, all ethnicities that they can live together in a peaceful way. And it is an alternative to capitalism and to patriarchy.

ISIS is massacring all minorities like Ezidis, Turkmens, Christians, and many others in the Middle East. Just a month ago the Ezidis of Sinjar were slaughtered. Together with the USA, Turkey, and other powers, ISIS desires to end particularly this alternative life that these women have made possible.

As we all may know, when Nazis carried out the genocide against Jewish people in the camps, although not the entire world was aware of what was happening in Nazi Germany, but some countries were and they chose to remain silent because of some bloody political tactics. Israel has killed thousands of Palestinians again and again and the last was the Gaza massacre. International powers have condoned the war crimes Israel committed again because of their bloody political interests. In 1990s the international powers did nothing except pretending they were doing something while the Serbian Army was raping, killing, and torturing women. And now in the Middle East, ISIS is executing a gruesome war. ISIS members are raping women, executing incomprehensible atrocity against women. And international powers pretend to do something but actually they are waiting for ISIS to end this alternative life in Rojava led by Kurdish women. These international powers along with our country Turkey are trying to sacrifice Kobanî for some political tactics, and Turkey is going further and directly supporting ISIS members. Turkey wants to make Rojava a buffer zone by evacuating just like Israel did for Palestinian land. Ironically, these are feast days in the Muslim world but actually there is nothing to celebrate under these painful circumstances.

In all wars it is always women's lives and gains which have been sacrificed for some political tactics. We as women all around the world cannot let history repeat itself. We all have to defend Kurdish women in Rojava, otherwise the history of women's struggle will not forgive us. Even if the lives of these women who have created an alternative life in Rojava do not matter for the states and the powerful, these lives must be a matter for us who are struggling for a better life for women.

It is a historical responsibility for women's rights activists, for feminists, for LGBT people, for socialist women and Muslim women all around the world.

WE CANNOT GO ON WITH OUR LIVES AS IF NOTHING IS HAPPENING! WE SHOULD RAISE OUR VOICE AGAINST THIS MASSACRE OF ISIS AGAINST KURDISH WOMEN EVERYWHERE WE LIVE BY ALL MEANS. WE SHOULD RAISE OUR VOICE. WE SHOULD DEFEND THESE WOMEN. WE SHOULD RISE UP.

The following is a call for widespread public support
written by the Administration of Kobanî Canton. It was
released internationally by the Information & Relations
Center of the PYD, Media & Public Affairs Office (Europe)
and is dated 11/1/2014.

A Call for the Dream of Freedom

KOBANÎ, THE SMALL CITY ON THE SYRIA-TURKEY BORDER, forms a part of the civilization of Mesopotamia and is inspired by the long-standing human values that came into existence in Mesopotamia.

During the Syrian people's revolution, Kobanî was the first area in the west of Kurdistan (Rojava) that was liberated from control of the Baath regime. Practically, that was the first step toward establishing the democratic system in Rojava. This system has the potential to offer a model for a future democratic, pluralistic, and decentralized Syria. Kobanî became a safe haven for Syrian IDPs [internally displaced persons] who fled their homes during the bloody civil war. As a result, Kobanî has become a target of the enemies of democracy, freedom, and the values of humanity.

Since mid-2013, Kobanî has been facing a brutal blockade and aggression. These difficult conditions worsened from September 15th when Islamic State terrorists have been attempting to commit massacres against civilians. To prevent this murderous onslaught, the People's Protection Units (YPG), Women's Protection Units (YPJ), and residents of Kobanî have engaged in a legitimate act of self-defense against the barbaric forces of IS.

Islamic State (IS) terrorists are enemies of humanity and its cherished values of democracy, peace, pluralism, and solidarity. The IS represents a culture of death and destruction and engages in heinous crimes such as the beheading of civilians. They have beheaded American, British, and Russian citizens as well as thousands of defenseless Yazidis, Christians, Kurds, Turkmen, and Arabs. The Islamic State has committed acts of genocide in Deir al-Zoor, Mosul, Sinjar, Telaafar, and recently in Kobanî. No one can predict who their next group of victims will be. The group openly boasts about liberating Europe and the whole world.

We believe this murderous group must be stopped by whatever means possible and those who support and finance them should be held accountable. By defending Kobanî, the forces there are defending the human values that bind us all together.

Kobanî will continue its resistance and it calls upon all those who believe in our shared human values to offer their assistance. The self-defense fighters in Kobanî are fulfilling a historic role by fighting against the forces of darkness and they need the support of the civilized world in this endeavor. It is clear that the fall of Kobanî would mark a great blow to our common human values and the cause of peace, democracy, and progress all over the world. We are certain that through the support of democratic forces our victory can be achieved. All jihadist organizations and their sources of funding and support must be targeted as a key step toward eliminating them, in particular IS.

We, in Kobanî, thank you for your support as we struggle for the survival of our democratic experiment. With the help of those who believe in democracy, peace, and brotherhood of nations, we will be victorious.

The following is an essay by Dilar Dirik, a Kurdish activist. The essay describes not only the women's movement in Rojava, but the ways in which it has been distorted by western media and ideologues.

The Women's Revolution in Rojava:
Defeating Fascism by Constructing an Alternative Society

THE RESISTANCE AGAINST THE ISLAMIC STATE IN KOBANÊ HAS woken the world to the cause of Kurdish women. Typical of the media's myopia, instead of considering the radical implications of women taking up arms in a patriarchal society—especially against a group that systematically rapes and sells women as sex-slaves—even fashion magazines appropriate the struggle of Kurdish women for their own sensationalist purposes today. Reporters often pick the most "attractive" fighters for interviews and exoticise them as "badass" Amazons. The truth is, no matter how fascinating it is—from an orientalist perspective—to discover a women's revolution among Kurds, my generation grew up recognising women fighters as a natural element of our identity.

The People's Defence Forces (YPG) and the Women's Defence Units (YPJ) from Rojava (mainly Kurdish populated regions in northern Syria) have been fighting the so-called Islamic State for two years and now lead an epic resistance in the town of Kobanî. An estimated 35 percent—around 15,000 fighters—are women. Founded in 2013 as an autonomous women's army, the YPJ conducts independent operations and trainings. There are several hundred women's battalions across Rojava.

But what are the political motivations of these women? Why did Kobanê not fall? The answer is that a radical social revolution accompanies their rifles of self-defense…

First off, the meaning of women picking up guns against ISIS must be analyzed with the patriarchal implications of war and militarism, as well as the systematic nature of ISIS's war on women. In war, women are usually perceived as passive parts of the lands that men protect, while sexual violence is systematically used as a war tool to "dominate" and "humiliate" the enemy. Being a militant is seen as "unwomanly"; it crosses social boundaries, it shakes the foundations of the status quo. War is seen as a man's issue—started, led, and ended by men. So it is the "woman" part of "woman fighter" which causes this general discomfort. Even though traditional gender roles often essentialize and idealize women as saints, the punishment is vicious once women violate these assigned roles. That is also the reason why many struggling women, everywhere in the world, are subject to sexualized violence as combatants in war and as political prisoners. As many feminists have pointed out, rape and sexual violence hardly have anything to do with sexual desire, but are tools of power to dominate and force one's will over the other. In the context of militant women, the aim of sexualized violence, physical or verbal, is to punish them for stepping into a sphere reserved for male privilege.

Militant Kurdish women (currently) fight against the Turkish state, the second largest NATO army with its hyper-masculine military structure and a prime minister that appeals to women to bear at least three children; the Iranian regime, which dehumanizes women supposedly in the name of Islam; the Syrian regime, whose army systematically uses rape as part of their war strategy; and jihadists like ISIS. But further, they fight against the excruciating patriarchy in Kurdish society itself. Against child marriage, forced marriage, honor killings, domestic violence, and rape culture.

ISIS launched an explicit war on women through abductions, forced marriages, rape, and sex slavery. This systematic destruction of women is a specific form of violence: *feminicide*. Fighting women are punished for violating a perceived sphere of male privilege via sexualized violence. So, for ISIS-members , who have declared it as "halal" to rape enemy women and who are promised 72 virgins in paradise for their atrocities, militant women are indeed the ultimate enemy.

But considering that—apart from the explicit gendered nature of war and violence—around the world, women often play key roles in freedom struggles but are abandoned once "liberation" or "revolution" is perceived to be achieved and traditional gender roles make a comeback, supposedly to reestablish "normal" civil life, what can we learn about liberation from a radical standpoint?

The experience of Kurdish women with multi-layered oppression perpetuated by the status quo created consciousness of the fact that different forms of oppression are interrelated and constituted a starting point for the ideology that now drives the resistance in the three cantons in Rojava that were declared in January 2014 as autonomous, of which Kobanê is one. It is a resistance which resonates with struggling people worldwide, who claim the cause as their own.

So what are the politics behind Kurdish women's resistance?

"We don't want the world to know us because of our guns, but because of our ideas," says Sozda, a YPJ commander in Amûde, and points at the pictures on their common room's walls: PKK guerrilla fighters and Abdullah Öcalan, the imprisoned ideological representative of the movement. "We are not just women fighting ISIS. We struggle to change the society's mentality and show the world what women are capable of." Though there is no organic tie between the PKK and the Rojava administration, the political ideology is shared.

The PKK, founded in 1978, started a guerrilla war against the Turkish state in 1984. Initially aiming at an independent Kurdistan, it long moved beyond statehood and nationalism, both of which it now critiques as inherently oppressive and hegemonic, and advocates an alternative liberationist project in the form of inclusive, feminist, radical democracy and regional autonomy: "democratic confederalism" based on gender equality, ecology, and grassroots-democracy for all ethnic, cultural, linguistic, and religious groups.

Abdullah Öcalan explicitly states that patriarchy along with capitalism and the state lie at the roots of oppression, domination, and power: *"Man is a system. The male has become a state and turned this into the dominant culture. Class and sexual oppression develop together; masculinity has generated ruling gender, ruling class, and ruling state."* (Öcalan 2013) He emphasizes the need for autonomous and conscious feminist struggle: *"Woman's freedom cannot just be assumed once a society has obtained general freedom and equality."* (Öcalan 2013) PKK cadres attend seminars to challenge patriarchy and advocate gender equality to transform men's sense of privilege and entitlement. Öcalan makes the connection between different institutions of power clear: *"All the power and state ideologies stem from sexist attitudes and behaviour[...]. Without women's slavery none of the other types of slavery can exist let alone develop. Capitalism and nation-state denote the most institutionalized dominant male. More boldly and openly spoken: capitalism and nation-state are the monopolism of the despotic and exploitative male".* (Öcalan 2011) The women's movement independently produces sophisticated theories and critiques as well, but it is striking that a male leader of a Middle Eastern liberation struggle places women's liberation as a critical measure of freedom. Only when reading and understanding this movement's position and its corresponding actions is it possible to grasp the mass mobilization of women in Kobanê. It did not emerge out of nothing, but is based on a rooted tradition with a determined set of principles.

The PKK splits administration equally between one woman and one man, from party presidencies down to neighborhood councils, through its co-chair principle. Beyond providing women and men with equal decision-making power, the co-chair concept aims to decentralize power, prevent monopolism, and promote consensus-finding. The women's movement is autonomously organized, socially, politically, militarily. While these organizational principles seek to guarantee women representation, massive social and political mobilization aims to raise society's consciousness so that it internalizes the advocated principles. Influenced by the PKK's feminist stance, the majority of women in the Turkish parliament and municipal administrations are Kurdish. Together with the YPG/YPJ, PKK units were key to creating a safety corridor to rescue the Yazidis in the Sinjar Mountains in August. Some PKK women died defending Makhmour in Iraqi Kurdistan alongside male peshmerga fighters.

Inspired by these principles, the Rojava cantons enforce co-presidencies and quotas and they created women's defense units, women's communes, academies, tribunals, and cooperatives. The women's movement Yekîtiya Star is autonomously organized in all walks of life, from defense to economy to education to health. Autonomous women's councils exist parallel to the people's councils and can veto the latter's decisions. Laws aim to eliminate gender-based discrimination. Men committing violence against women are not supposed to be part of the administration. In the midst of war, one of the governance's first acts was to criminalize forced marriages, domestic violence, honor killings, polygamy, child marriage, and bride price. Many non-Kurdish women, especially Arabs and Syriacs, join the armed ranks and administration in Rojava and are all encouraged to organize autonomously as well. In all areas of life, including in the internal security forces (asayish) and the YPJ and YPG (people's defense units), gender equality is a central part of education and training.

While some columnists arrogantly claimed that women in Kobanê fight "for western values," women's academies in Rojava critique the notion that women in the west are more liberated than them or that the west has a monopoly on values like gender equality. "There is no individual freedom if the whole of society is enslaved." In public seminars, women come up with their own critiques of the social sciences and propose ways of liberating knowledge from power. Yet this popular and explicitly feminist social revolution is completely ignored by mainstream media.

"Our struggle is not just to defend our land", YPJ commander Jiyan Afrin explains. "We as women, take part in all walks of life, whether fighting against ISIS or combating discrimination and violence against women. We are trying to mobilize and be the authors of our own liberation".

What liberation?

The experience of the Kurdish women's movement illustrates that for meaningful social revolution, concepts of liberation must be freed from the parameters of the status quo. For instance, nationalism is a gendered, patriarchal concept. Its premises limit struggles for justice. Similarly, the idea of a nation-state perpetuates the dominant oppressive hegemonic system. Rather than subscribing to these concepts, liberation should be seen as a never-ending struggle, a quest to build an ethical society, solidarity between communities, and social justice. Hence, rather than being a rights-based side issue that puts the burden on women, women's liberation and equality of all genders become a matter of responsibility for all of society, because they become measures of defining society's ethics and freedom. For a radical and revolutionary freedom struggle, women's liberation must be a central aim, but also an active method in the process. Political participation must move beyond voting and rights and must be radically reclaimed by the people.

In an era in which female policy makers feed unjust wars in third world countries by pleading to "save the poor oppressed women," along with racist, chauvinist groups that seem to believe to contribute to the cause of Middle Eastern women through sensationalist egocentric actions they consider as radical, and in which extreme individualism and consumerism are propagated as emancipation and empowerment, the struggling women in Kobanê contributed to rearticulating radical feminism by refusing to comply with the premises of the global patriarchal capitalist nation-state order, by reclaiming legitimate self-defense, dissociating the monopoly of power from the state, and by fighting a brutal force not on behalf of imperialists, but in order to create their own terms of liberation.

From inside Kobanê, YPJ fighter Amara Cudî tells me via internet: "Once again, the Kurds appeared on history's stage. But this time with a system of self-defense and self-governance, especially for women, who may now, after millennia, write their own history for the first time. It is our philosophical views that made us women conscious of the fact that we can only live by resisting. If we cannot defend and liberate ourselves, we cannot defend or liberate others. Our revolution goes far beyond this war. In order to succeed is, it vital to know what you fight for."

Without this collective effort to raise society's consciousness, to transform formerly silenced people into political subjects, Kobanê would not have been able to resist for this long. That is why the ideological and political mobilization of the population of Rojava cannot be treated in isolation of their victories against ISIS—genuine revolution must first challenge society's mentality. Thus, the women's fight against ISIS is not only militarily, but also philosophically an existential one. They not only resist against feminicidal ISIS, but also the patriarchy and rape culture prevalent among their own community. After all, ISIS exploits the concept of "honor" in the region, constructed around women's bodies and sexualities. Thus, a large banner in the city centre of Qamishlo declares: "We will defeat the attacks of ISIS by guaranteeing the freedom of women in the Middle East."

One does not need to like the PKK, but one cannot appropriate Kobanê's resistance, while denying the thought behind it, and yet claim solidarity with the brave women fighting ISIS. You cannot write the epos of Kobanê's women without reading the life of Sakine Cansiz, a co-founder of the PKK, who led a prison uprising in Turkey and spat at her torturer's face, later on adding "As a militant of a just cause, I was afraid to say 'ah.'" She was murdered along with Fidan Dogan and Leyla Saylemez on January 9th, 2013 in the heart of Paris. Women like her paved the way to the fight against ISIS—women, labeled as prostitutes, terrorists, and confused irrational evil witches prior to the rise of ISIS, because they were fighting NATO-member Turkey. Today, Rojava's women decorate their rooms with photos of their comrades Sakine, Fidan, and Leyla.

The de-politicization of the struggle in Kobanê robs the fighters of their agency and takes the collective mobilization out of context for the interest of the coalition, which consists of states that ignored and marginalized the resistance of Rojava against ISIS for two years and which previously provided weapons to those now forming the same murderous group.

Solidarity with Kobanê's women means to actually care about their politics. It means to challenge the UN, NATO, unjust wars, patriarchy, capitalism, political religion, global arms trade, nationalism, sectarianism, the state-paradigm, environmental destruction—the pillars of the system that caused this situation to begin with. Do not allow those who created the dark, violent shadows over the Middle East, which led up to the rise of ISIS, pretend to be the good guys. Supporting the women in Kobanê means getting up and spreading the revolution.

References:

Öcalan, Abdullah, 2011, *Democratic Confederalism* (Cologne: Transmedia Publishing Ltd.).

Öcalan, Abdullah, 2013, *Liberating Life: Woman's Revolution* (Cologne: Transmedia Publishing Ltd.).

With the implicit support of the Iraqi Kurdish KDP, border ditches were dug on the border between KRG (Kurdish Iraq) and Rojava. The following is a statement on the matter from Rojava, requesting better solidarity from Kurdish Iraq. It was released by the co-presidency of the KCK in October 2014

Defend the Unified Rojava Revolution

T HE ROJAVA REVOLUTION IS A SOURCE OF INSPIRATION AND motivation for all Kurds. The uprising of one part of Kurdistan and the establishment of a free and democratic life there is a very valuable development. So, possible problems should be settled through dialogue and mutual understanding. The trench digging is a negative development for the Kurds while it is seemingly pleasing the enemies of the Kurds, for they have always benefited from the divisions and problems amongst the Kurds. Therefore, the problems should be resolved through political means without giving way to any further tension and division. No solution other than dialogue and political means should be preferred. In today's modern world, where different communities and states accommodate their differences through dialogue and political means, the Kurds, too, should follow such methods in settling their differences.

The entire Kurdish people, political groups, and political parties have obligations and responsibilities towards the Rojava revolution. This is what is expected of the KDP and KRG administration too. All the Kurds expect the KRG administration to feel itself responsible towards the Rojava administration and settle their differences politically, based on dialogue and mutual understanding. Therefore, at a time when everybody is looking forward to the elimination of barbed wires and walls that divide Kurdistan, digging trenches on the Rojava border is quite an astonishing move. All Kurds expect the KDP to quit such moves, as the Rojava people are negatively affected by the recent political tensions. At a time when many internationally known intellectuals, writers, and politicians are calling for solidarity with the Rojava revolution, the KDP is also expected to give political support to the Rojava revolution.

While many internationally distinguished personalities have entered into solidarity with the Rojava revolution, our people and the political forces in all parts of Kurdistan should protect the revolution. It's high time to embrace and defend the Rojava revolution. The terrorist bandits, backed by many regional and international forces, are attacking the Rojava revolution; this revolution should not be left alone. The support for the Rojava revolution should not be limited to material or spiritual help only; everybody should help defend it. Not only the Kurdish people, but also all the peoples in the world and the democratic and revolutionary forces should side with the Rojava revolution.

The people of Rojava have made such a revolutionary move that it will not only change the fate of Syria, but also determine the fate of the entire Middle East. As the Kurds are establishing a free and democratic community for themselves, they have at the same time taken great steps towards transforming Syria into a free and democratic country. As it has already been observed, this revolution will influence the whole Middle East.

As we highlight our support for the Rojava revolution which has displayed a great multi-dimensional resistance in recent days, we call on the entire Kurdish people, the Kurdish political parties and democratic forces to support and side with the Rojava revolution.

The following piece is a translation of "Rojava direnişi ulus-üstü bir direniştir," which was written by Ali Haydar Kaytan, one of the founding members of the PKK. It was first published in October 2014 in *Özgür Gündem* [English: *Free Agenda*], a Turkish weekly paper that has been banned multiple times for supporting the PKK.

The Resistance In Rojava Is A Super-National Resistance

THERE IS NO NEED FOR ORACLES. THE FATE OF OUR REGION, the cradle of humanity and civilization, is being decided in Kobanê. Will the wild beasts be let off their chains or will greater humanity prevail? This will become clear in the honorable battle in Kobanê.

In the fight between freedom and slavery which has been continuing for a thousand years one of these two contradictory tendencies will suffer a defeat at the hands of the other. Either the honor of humanity will come to predominance and will open the door for freedom and democracy. In which case all identities and cultures in this ancient geography of ours will have the chance to express themselves freely and live together in brotherhood. And women, who are history's oldest oppressed gender, class, and nation, will begin to build a world of freedom and peace. Or the wild beasts will take the upper hand and freedom and democracy will once again remain a dream. Even if it is not certain in what direction the day's developments are going, this is the obvious reality.

Everything indicates that it is not only Kurdistan but our entire region that is passing through an extraordinary period. To attempt to confront these extraordinary times with normal measures of struggle is to consign oneself to failure. For our methods of struggle to be suitable to the character of the times they must be extraordinary. However we can turn the historical developments of such a war to our benefit by finding and implementing the most productive methods of struggle. What is important here is the organization of a relentless resistance struggle alongside that of the superhuman resistance in Kobanê. Success is conditional on taking as a basic principle a kind of action that relies on organized and conscious communities instead of a temporary and passing explosion of rage.

Actions need organization and organization needs action. That up until now there have been deficiencies in this area is apparent. Even so, the reality of the people who rose up in solidarity with Kobanê has presented us with great opportunities to create unity of action through organization.

Everyone knows very well what the AKP (Turkey's ruling, reactionary Justice and Development Party) is imagining and what it wants to do. The Davutoğlu government wants above all to have Kobanê fall by providing all kinds of support to the ISIS gangs. However the fall [of Kobanê] is only the opening part of this plan. Behind this are designs to crush the whole of Rojava using ISIS. In fact the new President Erdoğan has expressed this openly. He said that after Kobanê next in line was Afrin, Serêkani, and Hasekê. In fact he has drawn up a verifiable road map for them. For Erdoğan to speak like this is entirely normal, because it is Turkish officers from the Special War Department that are running the disgusting war in Kobanê. It is obvious to those interested in Rojava that ISIS has become an extension of the AKP. That the AKP are attacking Kurds instead of facing the Assad regime which the AKP wants to topple so badly is proof of this.

It is necessary for us to repeat ourselves insistently: The AKP's concern is not with solving the Kurdish issue, but with *solving* the Kurdish Freedom Movement and removing the Kurdish reality. With both the presidency and the de facto leadership of the AKP under his control, Tayyip Erdoğan has not changed at all. The man who once said "if you don't think about it there won't be any Kurdish problem" is still at the same place. In this sense there was never anything like the "solution process." The AKP and its leadership, in the common parlance, put on a song and dance and took the process as period to prepare for their own sinister goals. Against this leader Öcalan showed great effort in order to pull them toward a real democratic solution. He knew how to remain patient even in those places where patience was exhausted and never pulled back from a position advocating democracy and peace. In short, we are indebted to leader Öcalan for the period of no clashes in Kurdistan and Turkey which has lasted until today.

Now the Kurdish people are taking their fate into their own hands. As the people of North Kurdistan take ownership of Kobanê they are intrinsically taking ownership of their own fate. They want to develop a solution themselves and for this reason they are being martyred. As these lines are being written, fourteen of our people have already lost their lives in the resistance. Everything has become quite open: the response of the AKP government to Kurds pouring onto the streets to support their brothers and sisters in Rojava has been to spill blood. ISIS and its local partners have taken a stand together with the AKP police and opened fire on the people who had taken part in the serhildan (uprising). Under these circumstances it is unavoidable that the people develop their own effective measures to defend themselves. The foundation of the defense of the people is organization and the foundational responsibility of responding in the moment of attack falls to the youth.

The AKP government, which had proclaimed its distance from the era of Turkey's coups, is now applying measures that remind one of the coup era in Kurdistan. In order to drive the people from the squares the police are acting in conjunction with soldiers, they are declaring it illegal to go out onto the streets and are implementing measures appropriate to martial law. In order to preserve their own hegemony they are calling upon all kinds of unlawfulness. They do not want to allow anything like an opposition to exist. They look at any oppositional voice, any demand from the people, any position taken against their theft and despotism as an attempted coup and begin to attack it. Now is the time to say stop. The squares, the avenues and streets—they do not belong to the AKP police, nor the local partners of ISIS, nor to the soldiers, but to the people. It should be them who pulls back off the streets and not the people. Life is the highest value and its meaning derives from its willingness to make all kinds of sacrifice.

All the forces which are on the side of freedom, democracy, and labor in Turkey should be in solidarity with the resistance of the Kurdish people in this process and must necessarily take responsibility for the Rojava Revolution. The only road to a solution is for all revolutionary-democratic forces to go into action with the spirit of super-national solidarity or solitary for the national-other; to limit AKP hegemony by uniting their forces and increasing the democratic struggle; and to establish the peace so longed for in Turkey. In particular the leftist forces should care to understand well the character of the process through which we are passing and fulfill their duty of leadership wholeheartedly. If they do not take responsibility for this duty and if they remain in a position of a spectator it is unavoidable that Turkey will slip into a new era of military coups. It is imperative that we free our people from the position of having to choose between coups and AKP hegemony. We are bound neither to the fascist hegemony of the AKP nor to a military-fascist coup. The only thing to which we are all obliged is to [work towards] our people living together in freedom and on equitable foundations.

The following is a campaign statement by Peace In Kurdistan, a UK-based campaigning organization that seeks a political resolution to the Kurdish question. It was released on October 16, 2014.

The Resistance of Kobanî will Triumph Over Tyranny

THE KURDISH PEOPLE OF KOBANÎ HAVE SHOWN TREMENDOUS courage and resilience in their resistance to the ISIS onslaught. The determination of the men and women to fight to defend the territory where they have established democratic self-rule has inspired people across the world.

The Kurds in Kobanî are defending the values of democracy, inclusiveness, respect for difference, and gender equality against a ruthlessly intolerant force that offers only an orgy of blood-letting, carnage, public executions, vile abuse of women, and even the repudiation of the right to education, learning, and independent thought. The Kurdish resistance, and in particular the brave men and women fighters of the People's Protection Units (YPG/YPJ), represent the hope that these humane values will triumph over a tyranny that would take humanity back to the dark ages. As such, the Kurds have received widespread respect.

In stark contrast, Turkey has been exposed for its duplicity and total unreliability as an ally in the coalition against the ISIS threat. Turkey's leaders from President Erdoğan downwards have preferred to bomb Kurdish camps, as they did on 14 October, rather than take swift and effective action against the murderous jihadists.

Turkey deployed 25 tanks near Mursitpinar near Kobanî on 6 October but no attempts have been made to intervene to save the strategically important city. Turkey has preferred to bargain with its allies to obtain support for the plan to establish a buffer zone in the Kurdish region of Syria and to force the US-led Coalition to launch an attack on Damascus, rather than to confront ISIS directly. We are supposed to believe that the "buffer zone" is designed to protect the civilians as a safe haven, but in reality the Kurds had secured their own safe haven for themselves in Rojava, of which Kobanî is a part. Rojava needs to be recognized as a democratic entity rather than support any attempt by Turkey to set up a buffer zone. How can Turkey be trusted following its at best lukewarm approach to confronting ISIS?

The Turks have not only stood by as passive onlookers on the border while the city of Kobanî has been besieged, they have consciously exacerbated the crisis in order to weaken the Kurdish resistance. Turkish leaders have resorted to making increasingly wild and unsubstantiated allegations about Kobanî and the motives of the Kurds.

Turkish troops have contributed towards the suffering of the civilian population of Kobanî by obstructing volunteers seeking to help defend the city.

They have closed the border to supplies and blocked Kurds from Turkey trying cross to Kobanî in an attempt to bolster the resistance. People throughout the world have watched on utterly aghast at Turkey's shocking actions and they have drawn their own conclusions. Many now see Turkey as acting in collusion with ISIS and share the outrage of the Kurds that this is a shameful and unforgivable act.

President Erdoğan's repeated assertions that the PKK is as much of a threat as ISIS, if not greater, are simply baffling and utterly unsubstantiated by the facts. But this seemingly perverse attitude does expose the deep seated animosities against Kurds held by large sections of the Turkish public and it has become clear that this extends right into the heart of government. Ankara perceives its strategic interests to be at risk from any success achieved by the Kurds in Syria because it will inspire the Kurds inside Turkey to demand similar rights. The self-rule experiment in the three Rojava cantons of Northern Syria must have filled Turkish policy makers with utter dismay and it seems that they have viewed the appearance of ISIS as an opportunity to destabilize Rojava if not to overturn it altogether. The intransigence displayed over Kobanî is a clear demonstration of such a malicious intent.

The Kobanî resistance and the associations, real or imagined, between Turkey and ISIS that have come to the forefront of the world's attention over recent weeks have radically transformed political perceptions. This has been a transformative moment in global politics. Many more people have now become all too aware of the ruthless calculations that determine Turkey's politics. Its preference of ISIS over the Kurds poses a challenge for even Turkey's staunchest defenders to support with any semblance of convincing arguments.

The Kurds, by contrast, have earned enormous respect for their fortitude and determination in putting up a resistance against ISIS for so long and so successfully given the huge odds stacked against them. ISIS is a formidable force; it is well funded, well-armed, and can count on some powerful supporters.

The remarkable support shown by Kurds in the UK and throughout Europe for Kobanî has had an enormous impact on changing public opinion. A momentum of support for the Kurds has been building up with more and more people convinced by their impressive stand against ISIS which is seen as an enemy of humanity.

The conflict between the Kurds and the Turkish state is at the root of the attitude of Turkey towards ISIS in the current crisis over Kobanî. A credible resolution to this conflict must entail decriminalizing the only party that truly represents the Kurds in Turkey and which is affiliated with the Kurdish resistance in Syria, namely the PKK. Erdoğan's attempt to characterize the PKK as another ISIS simply lacks all credibility and should not be given credence by members of the Coalition formed to fight ISIS, many of whom are Turkey's fellow NATO members.

There will ultimately remain no alternative to the peace process between Turkey and the Kurds despite the hostility shown by Erdoğan towards Kurdish interests in Rojava. Much more effective pressure must be brought to bear on Turkey to restart the peace process and take concrete steps to negotiate a political solution to the conflict which should include the delisting of the PKK and the release of Abdullah Öcalan.

The Kurds have earned their entitlement to be treated as equals in any negotiated peace. That's the central lesson that needs to be drawn from the siege of Kobanî and the inspirational Kurdish resistance to the tyranny of ISIS.

On *Newroz*, the Kurdish New Year's Day, March 20th, 2005, imprisoned PKK leader Abdullah Öcalan released a call for "Democratic Confederalism." In it, he described the basic idea of what has since become the basis for the Rojava revolution.

Call to support Democratic Confederalism

CURRENT EVENTS THROUGHOUT THE WORLD, INCLUDING THE Middle East, and the situation in Kurdistan have led to the conclusion that to develop and establish democratic confederalism is an unavoidable historical duty. To start to develop, promote and establish democratic confederalism on a new Newroz [New Year's] day is historically seen as a progressive, exciting, and liberating step.

Democratic confederalism of Kurdistan is not a state system, but a democratic system of the people without a state. With the women and youth at the forefront, it is a system in which all sectors of society will develop their own democratic organisations. It is a politics exercised by free and equal confederal citizens by electing their own free regional representatives. It is based on the principle of its own strength and expertise. It derives its power from the people and in all areas including its economy it will seek self-sufficiency.

Kurdish democratic confederalism draws its strength from the historical roots of its people, and the deep-rooted, rich cultural identity of Mesopotamia. It is based on the democratic communal structure of natural society. Throughout their whole history Kurds have favored clan systems and tribal confederations and struggled to resist centralized governments. Democratic confederalism is based on the reality of the people, the free life and the vast experience of democratic organization and structures which the PKK has fought for for over 30 years in all areas of the struggle, in particular in prisons and in the mountains with its thousands of martyrs.

Democratic confederalism aims and struggles to press for deep-rooted reforms in order to open the road to democracy and to remove any barriers facing democratisation. From now on, three laws will be applied in Kurdistan: EU Law, the law of the national government, and the democratic confederal law. So long as the national/international governments of Iran, Iraq, Turkey, and Syria respect the democratic confederal laws the Kurdish people will observe their laws and thereby common ground will be sought.

Democratic confederalism is based on the principle of the recognition and preservation of all cultural identities as well as the promotion of the right to freedom of expression. To this end, it seeks as its main task the resolution of the Kurdish question by democratic means, the recognition of the Kurdish identity on all levels and the development and furtherance of the Kurdish language and culture.

The principle of democratic confederalism promotes an ecological model of society. It is opposed to all forms of sexual oppression and aims to overcome it through the liberation struggle of the women. It seeks the establishment of democracy in all spheres of life of Kurdish society which is based on ecology and equality of the sexes and struggles against all forms of reaction and backwardness. It conjoins individual rights and freedoms with the development of democracy.

Democratic confederalism seeks the resolution of society's problems without resorting to violence and thus it is based on a policy of peace. It will use the right to legitimate self-defense against any attacks on its country, its people, its freedoms, and against any violation of its rights.

Democratic confederalism is the movement of the Kurdish people to establish their own democracy and system of society. It is the expression of a democratic society and transcends all national structures. It is based on the freedoms of political, social, economic, cultural, sexual, and ethnic rights. It strives for the unity of the different ecological and communal organizations and at the same time represents the governing organization as an expression of organized society. On this premise, I am calling upon all sectors of society, in particular all women and the youth, to set up their own democratic organizations and to govern themselves.

Democratic confederalism is the expression for the democratic unity of the Kurds who are spread in four countries and scattered throughout the world. It seeks the resolution of the internal problems of the Kurdish nation through democratic unity. It views the tendency to create a nation state based on nationalism as a continuation of an outdated understanding of the nation state. As these models will neither resolve the Kurdish question nor assist the Kurdish people in the development of Kurdish society I call on these forces to be open to democratisation and to join the confederation on the basis of democratic unity.

Democratic confederalism is based on a deep-rooted democratic understanding and sense of freedom; it makes no difference between peoples and defends the equality and freedom of all peoples. It replaces the centralist nation state based on borders. It is the basis for the unity of the peoples and democratic forces of the Middle East. It establishes its relationships with neighboring countries on the basis of equality and freedom of political, social, and cultural rights. To that end, I call on all regional peoples to unite within the democratic confederation and I call on the neighboring countries to adopt a democratic position.

Democratic confederalism is opposed to global imperialism and seeks the global democracy of peoples. It is a system in which all peoples and all humanity should be living in the 21st century. This will pave the way for global democratic confederalism and a new era. I call on humanity to create a new world under the umbrella of a global democratic confederalism.

I believe by announcing the formation of the KOMA KOMALEN KURDISTAN (KKK), as the expression of democratic confederalism and the unity of the Kurdish people, on this Newroz day 2005 we have established a new philosophy and way of life for our people. I call on all our people to establish their own democracy, to unite and to govern themselves under their own flag (on green background a yellow sun with a red star). I will carry this flag proudly and I will continue to carry out my duties as a leader. On this day of spring, a day closer to freedom than the days of springs in the past, I wish our people and the regional peoples a Happy Newroz. With kind regards.

The following is a statement released by the Halkevi Turkish and Kurdish Community Centre in London on February 14th, 2014.

Peace, Equality, and Self-determination:
The Kurds Take the Lead in Proposing a New Way for Syria

THE KURDISH EXPERIMENT IN DEMOCRATIC AUTONOMY IN Syria has taken important steps forward in recent weeks with the declaration of self-rule in the Rojava region amid massive popular celebrations. Despite having suffered brutal repression at the hands of Assad over many years, the Syrian Kurds have refrained from joining in the attempt to overthrow the regime by violent means and instead opted to defend themselves from threats from regime and rebel forces by exercising their right to self-determination. In doing so, the Kurds have defended the rights and freedoms of all communities residing within the Kurdish controlled region, repudiating sectarianism as utterly alien to their progressive democratic principles. This enlightened position stands in stark contrast to the divisive targeting of minorities and deliberate ethnic cleansing carried out by groups like Jabhat al-Nusra, whose onslaught continues to threaten civilians in Rojava and the relative peace that has been maintained there since the start of the conflict.

Saleh Muslim, co-chair of the PYD, has stated that Syrian Kurds do not support either the government or the rebel groups, but only seek to protect themselves from massacres and ethnic cleansing. Islamist militias have been waging a brutal ethnic cleansing on Kurdish villagers and have been responsible for atrocities and massacres against unarmed Kurdish civilians. "Those who attack us and our homes have no respect for democracy or freedom; they have no respect for anything," the Syrian Kurdish leader continued. "All that we have said and done from the very outset was to protect ourselves both from the regime and from these forces."

Bloody clashes continued over the summer near the Turkish border between the Syrian Kurds headed by the PYD and the al-Nusra Front threatening to destabilise the region and spill over into Turkey. In reaction, Foreign Minister Ahmet Davutoglu has warned that the country would not stand by if the conflict "poses a threat to Turkey's security."

Kurdish towns Tel-Aran and Tel-Hasel and its villages of Aleppo, have been under brutal attack, with hundreds of innocent Kurdish children, women, and elderly people murdered and ritually beheaded. In addition, hundreds of civilians have been taken hostage with their fate still unknown and thousands civilians forcibly fled their homes in horror at the violence from these armed terrorist groups, according to the PYD.

What needs intense scrutiny is the role of Turkey in fuelling the conflict in the Kurdish part of Syria. Despite Turkish official denials of giving support to groups like al-Nusra, Turkey's claims to be totally uninvolved cannot simply be accepted without question. There is also the issue of cross-border arms supplies coming from Turkish territory to these militant groups. These issues need to be investigated and stopped immediately.

Turkey has been prepared to enter into talks with Saleh Muslim, but has not ceased in its attempts to undermine the integrity of the Kurdish position inside Syria, alarmed by the self-government exercised by the Kurds in the country since the outbreak of the civil war, fearing that its example of freedom and democracy will spread to Turkey itself.

Syrian Kurds led by the PYD have put forward detailed and constructive proposals for a peaceful democratic transformation of Syria that preserves the ethnic diversity and secular character of the country. In November last year, plans were announced to establish an interim administration to govern the region, and on the eve of the Geneva II conference, on 21 January 2014, the Kurds officially declared autonomy. Three separate cantons in Cizîre, Kobanê, and Efrîn are being headed by a coalition of Kurds, Assyrians, Christians, Armenians, and Muslims, and a new Rojava Constitution has been drawn up in which the rights of the child and of women to full participation in political, economic, and social life is guaranteed. This new administration must be more widely supported as it represents a genuine people-led proposal for a peaceful future Syria. We support the right of the Kurds in Syria to exercise democratic self-government in the region.

We call for the release of any civilian hostages held by rebel groups and urge an immediate halt to the arms supplies to these factions who are turning their weapons on innocent civilians and carrying out war crimes. A team of experts needs to visit the Kurdish area to verify the reports of recent massacres, to compile evidence that will bring the perpetrators of this heinous act to justice.

Both the Istanbul-based Syrian National Council and their international supporters have repeatedly ignored calls for the Kurdish question to be included in the Geneva II peace talks and for the participation of the Kurdish bloc as an independent group. This is one reason why the talks have descended into farce; the only parties that genuinely represent the Syrian people are simply not present while international and regional players attempt to carve out a new Syria modelled on their own interests. They are also only now waking up to the very real threat that groups like Jabhat al-Nusra pose to the country, having tacitly encouraged, and even financially and logistically supported these groups for over two years. Whatever strategy Washington and its allies, including Turkey, might be seeking for a future Syria, the recognition of the democratic rights of the Kurds surely needs to be central; Kurdish rights must be protected and acknowledged along with those of the many religious and ethnic communities living in this extremely diverse country which historically has been one of the most multicultural countries in the Middle East.

We urge you to respond to the emergency appeal to defend the Kurds in Syria. They stand for the values of peace, freedom and democracy for all the peoples of Syria that the international community itself claims to uphold. The Kurds are calling for our support. We should not let them down.

The following is a statement that was released by the European branch of the Syrian PYD on June 10th, 2013.

Western Kurdistan and the Revolutionary Period

THE KURDISH PEOPLE IN WESTERN KURDISTAN (NORTHERN Syria) constitute a population of 3.5 million and make up around 15% of the Syrian population. Western Kurdistan is demographically pluralistic and is home to Kurds, Arabs, Yezîdî Kurds, Alawite Kurds, as well as Christians, Assyrians, Chaldeans and Armenians. The multi-ethnic and multicultural fabric of western Kurdistan has always lived in peace and harmony with one another. Since the beginning of the great Syrian revolution the Kurds rejected a militarization of the conflict and quickly denounced the brutal manner in which the regime cracked down on the peaceful protesters.

The Kurdish people rose in solidarity with the Syrian revolution and bitterly condemned the repressive ways of the regime. Very quickly the Kurdish protesters called for the overthrow of the regime, a position it has maintained ever since. It also condemned the increasingly strong engagement and intervention of external forces that tried, and still tries, to utilize the great cause of the Syrian revolution for their own narrow interests. Ever since the revolution the Kurds have focused on protecting themselves and their region from attacks by the Syrian regime and armed groups. These armed groups represent a myriad of forces ranging from Salafist jihadist and petty crooks to factions of Free Syrian Army. The protective measures undertaken by the Kurds, more notably by the Popular Protection Units (YPG) which are operating under the highest political body in western Kurdistan, the Supreme Kurdish Council (DBK) has largely exempted the Kurds from the horrors of current the civil/sectarian war. The Kurds have installed new institutions and organizations, effectively replacing the former political/social landscape of the Ba'ath-party. This has enabled them to spare western Kurdistan from political economic free-fall and given them the tools to meet the basic needs of the general population. It has enabled them to harbor the countless displaced (a couple of hundred thousand) people and to assist those in most need.

Kurdish cities have been attacked countless times. Armed groups, chauvinists, and fundamentalists, who refuse to recognize the pluralistic fabric of Syria, have attacked Serê Kaniyê, Til Temir, and more recently Efrîn, a city located in northwestern parts of Syria. For more than 10 days armed groups along with salafist elements have surrounded the city of Efrîn, effectively stopping the flow of goods, including medicine, baby milk, flour, vegetable oil, and fuel, to the city. This policy of starvation is having terrible effects on the population of Efrin ranging to about million after the massive inflow of internal refugees. However, they haven't been able to breach the defense of YPG.

It is our hope that the grave situation in Efrin will be discussed and highlighted in the Geneva II peace talks. We hope that the concerned parties will hear our message and we call upon the international community and the guardians of basic human rights, to take actions in order to put an end to the devastating siege on Efrin. It is our sincere hope that the question in western Kurdistan can be solved in a democratic and peaceful manner.

This interview first appeared in the Kurdish news agency *Fırat Haber Ajansı* (English: *Firat News Agency*) and then translated in April 2014 for the website The Rojava Report. It has been reproduced here with its introduction intact.

Rojava's Economic Model is a Communal Model

In a new interview for ANF, Seyit Evran has spoken with Professor Dr. Ahmet Yusuf, who was made President of the Committee on Economy and Trade of the Afrin Autonomous Canton following its proclamation of autonomy this past January. Dr. Yusuf spoke about the prevailing economic model in the world, and the attempt in Rojava to build an alternative economy around a social communal model as laid out by Abdullah Öcalan. "Because this model" Dr. Yusuf says, "is the model by which the history of humanity will be brought back to life our chances of winning are high." Evran's interview with Dr. Yusuf has been translated into English below.

Seyit Evran: *How do you assess the social and economic model set forth by the Kurdish leader Abdullah Öcalan?*

Dr. Ahmet Yusuf: Mr Öcalan's economic perspective, thought, and propositions are not of the "third course" [developed in the West]. Nor do I think they have much to do with politics. We can see this when we look at them together with the thinking which emerged in the West in the course of historical economic development. Here we can understand where Öcalan's thinking fits in.

The world experienced a revolution in 1492. In 1498 it experienced another. The results were hardly beneficial but they have come to be remembered as revolutions. Let us accept them and assess them as such. In 1492 Christopher Columbus discovered the Americas. In 1498 Vasco da Gama was exploring Africa and passing behind Africa was able to reach India. Following these two encounters a period of savagery and oppression begins on earth. The wealth of the locals whose land had been "discovered" were seized. The foundations of the capitalist nation-state were being laid in the flows of Mercantilism. The nation-state, whose foundations had been laid in this period, became much stronger during its classical period in the 19th Century. The savagery which emerged with this development was of its own creation. It also has the name of capitalism. It looked upon life, communities, societies, and nature only with the eyes of the colonialist. Externally it developed through oppression, colonialism, and pillage, while internally it did not recognize the right to life of the poorer classes. Representatives of the church also played a role in these developments, for example Robert Malthus. Economic developments in the world grew along this first course.

The second course began with the publication of the *Communist Manifesto* developed under the leadership of Karl Marx in the 1840s. Existing savagery and oppression in the market was to be taken from the capitalists and transferred to the state. The second course developed in opposition to the first. The 20th Century saw a little development in this direction but it was not able to produce a solution for the social or economic problems of humanity. Nor could it solve the problem of freedom for communities, peoples, and cultures. Communities were only considered with respect to economic factors. For that reason the problems of freedom, equality, and justice could not be solved. This [second] course was shaped by Marxist-Leninism. It became concrete in the guise of the Soviet Union. It saw some development. However it was also organized as a dictatorship of the Proletariat. Capitalist countries closed themselves against it in fear. They were seized with fear that communism would spread from Eastern to Western Europe. For this reason certain social and economic schools of thought founded in the West came out with a third course. This was a new course. Its goal was to obstruct the spread of Communism in Europe, to prevent it. They planned to accomplish this by return some of the rights seized from the poor and from workers during capitalism's development. This third course became stronger through the 1950s, 60s and 70s. This course created a beautiful life for the workers of Germany, France, and Switzerland. Workers became the bearers of other rights than just labor rights. In the Scandinavian countries workers achieved this at a very high level.

In 1991, with the fall of the Soviet Union, this course disappeared. Capitalism took back the rights which it had recognized for workers out of fear of communism one by one.

The course set out by the Kurdish People's Leader Abdullah Öcalan emerges in the 1990s after this collapse. It strengthened as it went forward. For that reason I don't think that calling it a third course quite fits. In fact it sounds as if it is an attempt to identify it with the third course that has collapsed and is disappearing [in the West]. This course, whose foundations were laid in the 1990s, became laid in more general terms after 1999. The details became clearer after 2007. Because in these years a crisis of capitalism was emerging. In my opinion this course is a fourth course as regards the economy. Not the third course. It is a course that rests on society, social development, life, and the organization of life. It is a course which comments on and evaluates Capitalism, Marxism, and the opinions of Rosa Luxembourg. It is a course which is against a monopoly economy. It is a course that will protect the existence of communities in so much that it is a course that pays attention to ecology to the utmost. It is a course that will find a solution for the social and economic problems of the people of the region and the world. Of course for this course to develop it must be well-presented. We cannot keep it to ourselves. We need to familiarize [others] with it through practical steps.

Evran: *Why were you particularly interested in Öcalan's ideas?*

Yusuf: In Economics we read about the ideas of Capitalism and Marxism. We read ideas produced by people from Western countries. They developed many different theories from which to approach our region but until now none of them have produced any positive results for the people or the peoples [of this region].

Following the collapse of the Abbasid dynasty not many substantial ideas were produced in the region and the situation remained more or less the same until the end of the 20th century. Towards the end of the 20th century Mr. Öcalan's perspective, thinking, theory, and ideas emerged as the free thinking of the region. It became an alternative to Western thinking. Practices were produced to resolve the region's problems both according to Western thinking and in keeping with the reality of the region—its spirit, its particularities, its traditions, its history and culture. Öcalan has commented on the work of Western academics, economic chairs, etc. as regards their perspectives, thoughts, and ideas about the region with a view from the region. And he selected from these that which would work for the region. From this perspective I see a chance of success. I have been able to look at the world economy from two windows. The first window is Western positivism and the second window is the window onto the region which Öcalan has opened in front of me.

Evran: *What are your short, medium, and long-term projects to solve the economic problems of the canton?*

Yusuf: We are have taken this course as our main principle in Afrin and all the cantons of Rojava and we are developing our economic projects along this line of thought. Taking this course as our foundation we are trying to organize our economy, to reinvigorate it and to develop it. This course is the course of the social communal economy.

We are meeting with people from all social backgrounds and walks of life. We get their views. We listen to their demands and wishes. Little by little we are developing our projects in accordance with these.

Therefore the economy which we want to create in the Afrin Canton will be a social economy. For that reason we are starting with cooperatives. We are starting with small units of production. We will develop an economy based on agriculture, that is to say production. We will base this mode of production on a foundation by which all the peoples of the region will be included and benefit from it. With such a step we aim to change the economic model in Syria. We will develop projects in which we consider the interests of all the people in Syria. At the same time we will have presented an economic model for the peoples of the region. These are our long term plans.

Carrying them out is not even that difficult. Because the economic infrastructure of our canton is very strong. It is home to rich lands on which all kinds of production can be carried out. There is a lot of manpower. And it is a hard-working, productive manpower.

Evran: *What are your urgent goals right now?*

Yusuf: We will begin by finding a solution to unemployment. We will find this in developing a thinking around production that is supported by the land. Because our economic model is a model which takes as its base a production based on the land and animal husbandry. We will encourage everyone to work their own lands based on the needs of the community. We will also develop animal husbandry. During the Baath regime period animal husbandry had almost been finished off. Animal products were coming to the Afrin Canton and its environs from the outside. It is still this way.

We will attempt to include regional capital investors in this process. But we will not allow them the opportunity to exploit the community and people or monopolize. The Afrin canton is an agricultural canton. For that reason we will solve the problems of our farmers and will contribute to the diversification of their production. We will build small production units, for example we will give more importance to the region's olive production which up until now has not been given importance. We will move towards small-scale industrialization in our region in which all olive products will be processed.

Evran: *Do you have any projects designed to develop economic and commercial relations with your neighbors?*

Yusuf: Of course there are. As we consider our possibilities there will be a need for a market for these products. At the same time there are things which must come from foreign markets into our region. We will attempt to go beyond this with trade. For this reason we will try to develop our relations with neighboring countries.

Right now we are experiencing certain difficulties that are a result of the problems being experienced in Syria more generally. For example our canton has received hundreds of thousands of refugees. Together with this came certain difficulties. We are trying to create job, production, and work opportunities for those just coming off the road. We are trying to provide opportunities for work with the small-scale production units we have opened. In order to go beyond this we are trying to develop relations with neighboring countries. We are trying to develop relations with Turkey. We will show them that the peoples of

Rojava will not be a problem for Turkey but on the contrary a benefit. We will also develop relations with our brother Arab peoples who are living through such difficulties. We will make them a partner in our economic model and projects for a solution. We are inviting all peoples and countries to come learn about the model which we want to implement. We do not want the English, French, or American model, we want to return, thanks to Mr. Öcalan, to a model that worked for our region for tens of thousands of years. We will succeed in this. Because there is no other model left to try on earth. Because this model is the model by which the history of humanity will be brought back to life our chances of winning are high.

Dr. Yusuf was born in Atmana village in the Raco district of Afrin in 1962. He began primary school in his village and went to Raco to study after the 6th grade. Following the 12th grade Dr. Yusuf went to Aleppo to study as there were no educational opportunities in Rojava. He married in 1991 and is the father of two children.Dr. Yusuf has worked in different universities around Rojava and Syria.

In December 2014, an international delegation of academics visited the Cizîrê canton in Rojava to learn about the revolution. This is Becky's reportback.

A Revolution in Daily Life:
Cizîrê Canton, Rojava

The relation of exploitation contains, in an immanent way, a direct relation of domination, of subjection, and of social and police control. But when one takes the relation of domination, of subjection, as the totality of the relation of exploitation, the part for the whole, then one loses sight of the relation of exploitation and of the classes. The moment of coercion taken as starting point and posited as the totality of the relation between the individual and society inevitably lapses into the point of view of the isolated individual and the critique of everyday life.
—*Theorie Communiste*[1]

A CROSS THE DOMAINS OF GOVERNMENT IN THE CANTON OF Cizîrê, people are working, mostly on a voluntary basis, to make ambitious transformations to society. Doctors want to build a modern free healthcare system but also, they told us, to collect and disseminate suppressed local knowledge about healing and to change the conditions of life in general. They aim, they said, to build a way of life free of the separations—between people and between people and nature—that drive physical and mental illness. Academics want to orient education to ongoing social problems. They plan, they said, to abandon exams and destroy divides between teachers and students and between established disciplines. The new discipline of "jinology" (the science of women) constructs an alternative account of mythology, psychology, science, and history. Always and everywhere, we were told, women are the main economic actors and those with responsibility for "ethics and aesthetics," "freedom and beauty," "content and form." The revolution aims to overcome the limits placed on these activities when the State is taken as a model for power.

It was repeated to us again and again that the coexistence and coordination of changing cross-cutting pre-existing identities is to replace "one flag, one language, and one nation." The new administration is composed of quotas of representatives from Kurdish, Arab, and Assyrian communities, nominated according to their own practices. Although the militias and security forces are ethnically mixed, Assyrian groups have their own battalions. Everyday life has changed most for women, who were previously restricted to a life indoors. Although the streets are still mainly the province of men, women have set up their own education structures and their own local councils. All mixed political bodies must be 40% women and all co-representatives must include one woman. Women are thus both autonomously organized within the revolution and its archetypal subjects. The billboards in Qamislo show the YPJ's women fighters more than YPG's male ones. "We will defend you," one reads.

Members of the YPJ spoke to us about the non-hierarchical organization that exists within the militias. There are elected commanders, they said, but they participate in all the activities of communal life in the same way as everyone else. But it's not all love and post-structuralism. Discipline is also an important part of the ethics and aesthetics of daily life. The women we saw being educated as security forces (asayish) were taught sitting in rows. It was a bit of a shock on the first day of our tour, to be greeted by a line of trainees in uniform, standing with perfect rigidity in a line doing that call and response thing armies do, precisely and very loud. YPG training videos, set to music, play on every TV. Even in the University, where young people live collectively, cooking and cleaning-up happened in a super-efficient way: tasks are performed efficiently, divided up between everyone, so that equality and horizontality and automatic discipline overlapped perfectly.

Another ethic and aesthetic ambiguity surrounds the significance of the PKK's Öcalan, or "Apo" (the name for him people more commonly write on walls and carve into their guns). His picture hangs on the wall in almost every room. The "libertarian turn" of the PKK, with which Rojava's PYD are affiliated—its renunciation of hierarchical structure among other things—was initiated by him. It is interesting to note, that it was also after a period spent in this region, before his arrest in 1999, although he is always attributed with coming up with the ideas. The other images that adorn walls, dashboards, and plants are those of martyrs—their faces against a colored background that denotes their organization. Is it significant that Öcalan is the only person still alive to be given this honor and a leader with whom no one can communicate directly and with no de facto power?

Weakening the state

The point of the revolution, many people told us, is not to replace one government with another, it is to end the rule of the state. The question, the co-president of the Kurdish National Congress put it, is "how to rule not with power but against power." State power is being dispersed in a number of ways. The education of people as Asayish is taking place on a large scale, with the aspiration that everyone will receive it. It is part of an attempt to diffuse the means of coercion to everybody. People's self-defense, we were told, is "so important that it can't be delegated." Through education (not only in the use of weapons but also in mediation, ethics, the history of Kurdistan, imperialism, the psychological war waged by popular culture, and the importance of education and self-critique), the fighter in charge of one training center told us, the aim is to finally abolish Asayish altogether.

The new administration (with a parliament and 22 ministries), appointed for now by various political parties and organizations but to be eventually be elected, has taken responsibility for some state functions. When in spring 2012, ISIS reached Rojava, anticipating the carnage of a confrontation between ISIS and Assad and seeing the opportunity in the situation, the Kurdish forces surrounded the Syrian state forces in Derik and negotiated their departure (without their weapons). After consultation with other political and social forces in the area, the same happened across Rojava. However, the Assad regime has not been completely ejected. In Qamislo, the largest city in Cizîrê, it still controls a small area which contains the airport. The old state also continues to operate in parallel with new structures. Syrian hospitals to the south still accept some of the very sick and the regime still pays some civil servant salaries including those of some teachers.

Meanwhile, the new administration is balanced by multiple autonomous elements. Separate from it, communes (weekly open neighborhood councils, with their own local defense units and sub-councils dedicated also to youth, women, politics, economy, public services, education, and health) and city and canton-level councils consisting of delegates elected by them, deal with immediate practical problems that can be resolved immediately. Both the administration and the communes were set up by TEV-DEM, a coalition of organizations including the PYD, co-ops, academies, women's and youth organizations, and sympathetic political parties. These organizations all have their own decision-making structures and sometimes their own education programs in their "cultural centers" "houses" and "academies". The result of all this is both that all political forces have complex, cross-cutting reliances on each other and that there are plenty of meetings to go around.

And communism?

Little existent agricultural or industrial production takes place in Rojava, despite its flat and fertile soil. The "bread basket" of Syria, most of its land has been owned by the State and used for mono-cropping wheat and extracting oil. Its Kurdish population often immigrated to southern cities to form a class faction working for lower wages. The new administration took the land and distributes portions of it to self-organized co-ops who are working to expand the farming of animals and to increase and diversify what is grown. It continues to extract some oil and to refine it into low quality diesel to sell in the canton and to distribute to co-ops and other institutions. What co-ops produce is sold either to the administration or in the bizarre administration price controls. The administration provides each household with a bread ration. Smuggling is huge.

Those overseeing these changes describe them simply as practical solutions to the problem of how to reproduce the population in the context of war and embargo. This is very different from how the immediate practical transformations to the domestic sphere were described. The women's militia, members of the YPJ told us, "opened a space for liberation": "You take part in life in a new way and, when you are with others, you realise that you are a power." And, they said, "when people saw us fighting alongside the men they also accepted us fighting against male-centric mentalities." There was no talk about how the positive empowerment came with the necessity of disrupting relations of exploitation and exchange. Perhaps this was because the people we were brought to talk to were mainly middle class, although this fact itself is also significant.

In some ways, opposition to the state is opposition to capital, on the level of its global force. The new administration opposes, as they see it, NATO in two forms: in one as Turkey-supported ISIS and in the other US and international capital (a category into which the KRG—where two ruling families now construct refugee camps along one side of their motorways and shopping centers along the other—also falls). They have no illusions about the motivations of those who give them military support: "Everyone, including the US now, portrays it as if we are on their side!" TEV-DEM laugh. But there is no opposition to value in its everyday form continuing to exist. Those that debunk the claims of over-enthusiastic western activists about the revolutionary nature of what is happening in Rojava are right to describe it instead as the building of a shield against today's war and most brutal oppression, using, as well as an army, a new kind of ideology replacing that of national liberation.[2]

The situation also has something in common with the sad trajectory of struggles around the world in the past few years. The state, now an agent of global capital, is seen as the guilty party by movements composed of middle as well as proletarian classes. Meanwhile, the nation is seen as the force to oppose it. Struggles rally under the ideology of citizenship (and the race and gender hierarchies this presupposes). The transformation taking place in Rojava rests to some extent on a radical Kurdish identity and on substantial middle classes contingent who, despite radical rhetoric, always have some interest in the continuity of capital and the state.

Yet, at the same time, it also shares something with the high points of the struggles of the crisis: its riots. In some ways the strategies employed in Rojava were born from analysis of the failure of riots: in 2004, only months after the PYD formed, an uprising of Kurds demanding political freedom from the Syrian state met not only with immediate torture, murder, and imprisonment but with a long period of brutal oppression. We decided, they remembered, we would not make the same mistakes again. What is taking place is not communisation.[3] But it is a real movement against state plunder and coercion— fighting both militarily on its borders and inwardly through the diffusion of power within them. The limits of the struggles in Rojava in this sense are those of struggles everywhere where the relation between labor power and capital has become a matter of repression and struggles that take that repression as a starting point. These struggles take place far from the strongholds of capital's reproduction and are not directed at over turning relations of exploitation. What will be interesting in Rojava, for now largely cut off from the force of global capital, is what struggles will emerge over relations of exploitation... over the distribution of land, over assignment to different kinds of work, over prices and wages, over imports and exports. What transformation of property and production relations will women demand as they return from the militias?

Notes

1 Theorie Communiste (2009) The Glass Floor
HTTP://LIBCOM.ORG/LIBRARY/
GLASS-FLOOR-THEORIE-COMMUNISTE

2 Il Lato Cattivo (2014) The Kurdish Question
HTTP://ENDNOTES.ORG.UK/EN/IL-LATO-CATTIVO-THE-KURDISH-QUESTION-ISIS-USA-ETC

3 SIC International Journal for Communisation (2011)
HTTP://SIC.COMMUNISATION.NET/

This interview was published in the October 2014 issue
of the Turkish anarchist journal *Meydan* [which is Turkish
for "public square"].

"We are Kawa against Dehaks"
An interview with the DAF on Kobanê

*For two years now the foundations of social revolution have
been being developed in Rojava, the west of Kurdistan. Bearing
this [in mind], it's hard to ignore the fact that the basis of the
attacks against Kobanê is the interest politics of the Turkish State
and global capitalism. Abdülmelik Yalcin and Merve Dilber
from Revolutionary Anarchist Action (DAF) were in the region
of Suruc, on the border with Kobanê, since the first day of the
resistance against the attempts to obscure the people's revolution, in
solidarity with the people of the region. We interviewed them on
the Kobanê Resistance and Rojava Revolution.*

Meydan: *Since the beginning of the Kobanê Resistance, you have
organized a lot of protests and made leaflets and posters. You
also participated in "the human chain border watch" that was
organized in the villages at Suruc, near the Kobanê border. What*

was your purpose of going there? Could you tell us about what you went through there?

M. D.: Due to the Rojava Revolution the borders between the parts of Kurdistan that fell within Syrian and Turkish territory started to melt away. The Turkish State even tried to build a wall to destroy this effect of the revolution. In the midst of the war, in the interest of global capitalism and states in the region, the Kurdish people in Syria took a step along the path that leads to social revolution. Thanks to this step a real front emerged that leads to the freedom of the people, and in Kobanê, a total attack against revolution was started by the hands of ISIS, the violent mob produced by global capitalism. As revolutionary anarchists, when we considered the situation in Kobanê and all of Rojava, it was impossible for us not to become directly involved in it. Whereas the borders between states were abolished, it is vital to be in solidarity with peoples resisting in Kobanê. We are at the 15th month of the Rojava Revolution. In these 15 months, we organized a lot of joint protests and made leafleting and wheatpasting actions. During the latest wave of attacks against the revolution in Kobanê, we similarly made a lot of leafleting and wheatpasting and also organized a lot of street protests. However we had to go to Kobanê border to salute the Kurdish people' struggle for freedom against the attacks of ISIS mob. In the night of 24 September we departed from Istanbul to the Kobanê border. We met our comrades who arrived a little bit earlier and together started our human chain border guard in Boydê village, in the west of Kobanê. There were hundreds of volunteers like us who came from different parts of Anatolia and Mesopotamia to the border forming a human chain along 25km of the borderline in different villages like Boydê, Bethê, Etmankê, and Dewşan. One of the aims of the human chain was to stop man, arms, and logistics support to ISIS from the Turkish State, whose support to ISIS is known by everyone. In the border villages the life itself has transformed into a communal life, despite the war conditions. Another aim of our border watch was to interfere [with border enforcement]in solidarity with the people of Kobanê, who had to escape from the attacks against Kobanê, who were delayed at the border for weeks and who were even attacked by Turkish military police forces (jandarma). In the first days of our border watch actions, we cut the wires and crossed to Kobanê together with people coming from Istanbul.

Meydan: *Could you please tell us what happened after you crossed the border to Kobanê?*

A.Y.: The moment we passed the border, we were greeted with huge enthusiasm. In the border villages of Kobanê, everyone, young and old, were on the streets. YPG and YPJ guerrillas saluted our elimination of borders by firing into air. We rallied in the streets of Kobanê. Later, we had conversations with people of Kobanê and the YPG/YPJ guerrillas who defend the revolution. It is very important that the borders between peoples that the states erected were smashed like this. This action which occurred in the conditions of war shows once more that uprisings and revolutions cannot be stopped by the borders of states.

Meydan: *There was a lot of news about people who participated in "the human chain border watch" and the rural population around the border being attacked by military police and regular cops.*

What does the Turkish State try to achieve with its bullying at the border? What do you think about it?

A.Y.: Yes, it is true that the policy of the Turkish State is to attack everyone who is involved in the border watch and who lives in the border villages, and everyone from Kobanê who tries to cross the border. Sometimes these attacks happen frequently and sometimes they last for days. It is obvious that each attack has its own excuse as well as its own purpose. We observed that during nearly every military (gendarme) attack, trucks transport some stuff to the other side of the border. We are not sure about the exact contents of these shipments to ISIS. However, we could understand by the power of the attacks that sometimes it was to let people cross the border to join ISIS, sometimes to send arms and in other times it was to provide ISIS with its daily needs. These shipments were sometimes carried by vehicles with official plate numbers and sometimes by gangs who conduct state-sponsored "smuggling." Moreover these state-sponsored gangs usurped the properties of the people of Kobanê who wait at the border. Military police on the other hand let people cross the border with a commission fee of 30 percent. The policies of the state against the local population have been the same for years. Due to the conditions of war, this policy has become much more visible now. The attacks at the border are conducted with the purpose of intimidating the people in border watch actions and the people of the border villages.

Meydan: *Although the Turkish State denies this, it was more or less known that it supports ISIS. However you say that now, even people who cross the border to join ISIS can easily be seen. So in* *this region it is not hidden that the Turkish State supports ISIS. How does this support work at the border?*

M. D.: The Turkish State insistently denied its support to ISIS. However, ironically, whenever it declared a denial, a new shipment was being organized at the border. A lot of these shipments were large enough to be easily observed. For example: different vehicles brought "assistance packages" to border. We were witnesses to the fact that tens of "service vehicles" with black windows crossed the border. Nobody really wonders what is inside these vehicles. We all know that the needs of ISIS are satisfied through this channel.

Meydan: *Would you please care to explain the historical and contemporary importance for the revolutionary anarchists of embracing the Kobanê Resistance and Rojava Revolution, especially at a time like this?*

A.Y.: The Kobanê Resistance and Rojava Revolution should not be considered as separate from the long history of Kurdish people's struggle for freedom. In the land we live in, the struggle of Kurdish people for freedom was called the "Kurdish problem." For years, it was misrepresented as a problem sourced by the people and not of the state. We say it again: this is the struggle of Kurdish people for freedom. The only problem here then is the state. Kurdish people have been fighting a struggle of existence against the destruction and denial politics of Republic of Turkey for years, and against other political powers in these lands for hundreds of years. This fight is given against the state and capitalism with the organized power of people. In the slogan "PKK is people, people are here," it's clear who this political agent is, which became distinct in each and every individual and who this organized power is. Ever since we solidified our perception into struggle, in different contexts, our relationship with Kurdish individuals and society and the organization of Kurdish people, have been mutual solidarity. We base this relationship on the perspective of peoples' struggle for freedom. In people's struggle for freedom, anarchist movements have always been catalyzers. In an age where socialism couldn't get out of Europe, when there were no theories called "Right of Nations Choosing Their Own Destiny," anarchist movements took different forms in different regions of world as people's fight for freedom. To understand this, it's enough see the influence of anarchism on people's struggles in a wide range from Indonesia to Mexico. Also, neither the revolution in Rojava, nor the struggle of Zapatistas in Chiapas fit into description of classical national freedom struggles. Nation as a political term obviously has the state by definition. Therefore while considering the peoples' struggle for stateless self-organizations, we need to keep a distance to the concept "nation." On the other hand our approach does not involve likening or similarizing the Kobanê Resistance to any other historical instances. Nowadays different groups mention different historical periods and liken the Kobanê Resistance to these instances. However, it must be known that the Kobanê Resistance is the Kobanê Resistance itself; and the Rojava Revolution is the Rojava Revolution itself. If one wants to associate the Rojava Revolution, which created the basis for social revolution, one can investigate the social revolution that realized in the Iberian Peninsula.

Meydan: *Although the resistance in Kobanê is happening outside of the borders of the Turkish State, solidarity demonstrations were* *held in every corner of the world. What is your evaluation of the effects of the Kobanê Resistance—well the Rojava Revolution, actually—on particularly Anatolia but also on the Middle East and also on a global level? What are your predictions related to these effects?*

M. D.: The calls for *serhildan* (Kurdish word for uprising) were answered in Anatolia, especially in cities in Kurdistan. Starting from the first night (of the demonstrations) everyone in the streets saluted the Kobanê Resistance and the Rojava Revolution against the ISIS gangs and their supporter the Turkish State. Especially in the cities of Kurdistan, the state attacked the people's serhildan with its law enforcement and paramilitary associates. The state with its Hizbulkontra (A word play connecting the words Hezbollah and Contra-T.N.) associates terrorized Kurdistan and killed 43 of our brothers. These massacres are indicating how much the Turkish State fears the Rojava revolution and the possibility that such a revolution could also generalize in its territory. Attacking with desperation out of fear, the Turkish State and global capitalism have another fear is of course related to Middle East region. In the Middle East, despite all the plans, depredation, and manufactured violence, social revolution still managed to emerge. This messed up all the plans of global capitalism and regional states. This is such an upheaval that despite all the depravations, social revolution could emerge in Rojava. This revolution is the answer to all the doubt of whether revolution can happen in this region and on a global level. It strengthened the confidence in revolution specifically for the people of this region but also on the global scale. The purpose of all social revolutions in history was to achieve a globally socialized revolution. In this perspective we called international anarchist groups to act in solidarity with the Kobanê Resistance and the Rojava Revolution. With our call for solidarity, anarchists from different parts of the world from Germany, to Athens, to Brussels, to Amsterdam, to Paris and to New York held demonstrations. We salute once more every anarchist organization that received our call, organized demonstrations related to our call, and those who stayed here with us in the human chain border watch.

Meydan: *Starting from the first days of ISIS's attack, the Turkish State-sponsored media made a lot of news that claimed Kobanê is about to fall. However, what they understand after more than one month now, is this: Kobanê won't fall! Yes, Kobanê did not and will not fall. We, as Meydan Newspaper, salute your solidarity with Kobanê. Is there anything else you want to add?*

M. D.: We, as revolutionary anarchists, witnessed, lived, and are still living the invincibleness of the confidence in revolution, even in the circumstances of war in our region. What is happening in Rojava is a social revolution! This social revolution, where the borders are abolished, states are being rendered powerless, plans of global capitalism are disturbed, will also generalize in our region. We invite every oppressed individual to look from the point of view of the oppressed. With this awareness we also invite them to support the organized struggle for social revolution. This is the only way to fertilize the seeds which were planted in Rojava and live the social revolution in wider regions. Long live the Kobanê Resistance! Long live the Rojava Revolution!

A report by social ecologist Janet Biehl, one of the members of the international delegation to the Cizîrê canton. This report was first published by *ROAR* magazine on December 16, 2014

Impressions of Rojava:
a report from the revolution

From December 1 to 9, I had the privilege of visiting Rojava as part of a delegation of academics from Austria, Germany, Norway, Turkey, the UK, and the US. We assembled in Erbil, Iraq, on November 29 and spent the next day learning about the petrostate known as the Kurdish Regional Government (KRG), with its oil politics, patronage politics, feuding parties (KDP and PUK), and apparent aspirations to emulate Dubai. We soon had enough and on Monday morning were relieved to drive to the Tigris, where we crossed the border into Syria and entered Rojava, the majority-Kurdish autonomous region of northern Syria.

The Tigris river channel was narrow, but the society we encountered on the far shore could not have been more different from the KRG: the spirit of a social and political revolution was in the air. As we disembarked, we were greeted by the Asayish, or civilian security forces of the revolution. The Asayish reject the label police, since police serve the state whereas they serve society.

Over the next nine days, we would explore Rojava's revolutionary self-government in an old-fashioned state of total immersion (we had no internet access to distract us). Our delegation's two organizers—Dilar Dirik (a talented PhD student at Cambridge University) and Devriş Çimen (head of Civaka Azad, the Kurdish Center for Public Information in Germany)—took us on an intensive tour of the various revolutionary institutions.

Rojava consists of three geographically non-contiguous cantons; we would see only the easternmost one, Cizîrê (or Jazira), due to the ongoing war with the Islamic State, which rages to the west, especially in Kobanî. But everywhere we were welcomed warmly.

Rojava's Third Way

At the outset, the deputy foreign minister, Amine Ossi, introduced us to the history of the revolution. The Syrian Ba'ath regime, a system of one-party rule, had long insisted that all Syrians were Arabs and attempted to "Arabize" the country's four million Kurds, suppressing their identity and stripping those who objected of their citizenship.

After Tunisian and Egyptian opposition groups mounted insurgencies during the Arab Spring in 2011, rebellious Syrians rose up too, initiating the civil war. In the summer of 2012, the regime's authority collapsed in Rojava, where the Kurds had little trouble persuading its officials to depart nonviolently.

Rojavans (I'll call them by that name because while they are mostly Kurds, they are also Arabs, Assyrians, Chechens, and others) then faced a choice of aligning themselves either with the regime that had persecuted them, or with the mostly Islamic militant opposition groups.

Rojava's Kurds being relatively secular, they refused both sides and decided instead to embark on a Third Way, based on the ideas of Abdullah Öcalan, the imprisoned Kurdish leader who rethought the Kurdish issue, the nature of revolution, and an alternative modernity to the nation-state and capitalism.

Initially, under his leadership, Kurds had fought for a state, but several decades ago, again under his leadership, their goal began to change: they now reject the state as a source of oppression and instead strive for self-government, for popular democracy. Drawing eclectically from sources in history, philosophy, politics, and anthropology, Öcalan proposed "Democratic Confederalism" as the name for the overarching program of bottom-up democracy, gender equality, ecology, and a cooperative economy. The implementation of those principles, in institutions not only of democratic self-government but also of economics, education, health and gender, is called Democratic Autonomy.

A Women's Revolution

Under their Third Way, Rojava's three cantons declared Democratic Autonomy and formally established it in a "social contract" (the non-statist term it uses instead of "constitution"). Under that program, they created a system of popular self-government, based in neighborhood commune assemblies (comprising several hundred households each), which anyone may attend, and with power rising from the bottom up through elected deputies to the city and cantonal levels.

When our delegation visited a Qamishlo neighborhood (Qamishlo being the largest city in the Cizîrê canton), we attended a meeting of a local people's council, where the electricity and matters relating to women, conflict resolution and families of martyrs were discussed. Men and women sat and participated together. Elsewhere in Qamishlo, we witnessed an assembly of women addressing problems particular to their gender.

Gender is of special importance to this project in human emancipation. We quickly realized that the Rojava Revolution is fundamentally a women's revolution. This part of the world is traditionally home to extreme patriarchal oppression: to be born female is to be at risk for violent abuse, childhood marriage, honor killings, polygamy, and more.

But today the women of Rojava have shaken off that tradition and participate fully in public life—at every level of politics and society. Institutional leadership consists not of one position but two, one male and one female official—for the sake of gender equality and also to keep power from concentrating into one person's hands.

Representatives of Yekitiya Star, the umbrella organization for women's groups, explained that women are essential to democracy—they even defined the antagonist of women's freedom, strikingly, not as patriarchy but as the nation-state and capitalist modernity. The women's revolution aims to free everyone. Women are to this revolution what the proletariat was to Marxist-Leninist revolutions of the past century. It has profoundly transformed not only women's status but every aspect of society.

Even the traditionally male-dominated strands of society, like the military, have been profoundly transformed. The people's protection units (YPG) have been joined by the YPJ—or women's protection units—whose images by now have become world famous. Together, the YPG and the YPJ are defending society against the jihadist forces of ISIS and Al-Nusra with Kalashnikovs and, perhaps equally formidably, a fierce intellectual and emotional commitment not only to their community's survival but to its political ideas and aspirations too.

When we visited a meeting of the YPJ, we were told that the fighters' education consists not only of training in practical matters like weapons but also in Democratic Autonomy. "We are fighting for our ideas," they emphasized at every turn. Two of the women who met with us had been injured in battle. One sat with an IV bag, another with a metal crutch—both were wincing in pain but had the fortitude and self-discipline to participate in our session.

Cooperation and Education

Rojavans fight for the survival of their community but above all, as the YPJ told us, for their ideas. They even put the successful implementation of democracy above ethnicity. Their social agreement affirms the inclusion of ethnic minorities (Arabs,

Chechens, Assyrians) and religions (Muslims, Christians, Yazidis), and Democratic Autonomy in practice seems to bend over backwards to include minorities, without imposing it on others against their will, leaving the door open to all.

When our delegation asked a group of Assyrians to tell us their challenges with Democratic Autonomy, they said they had none. In nine days we could not possibly have scoured Rojava for all problems, and our interlocutors candidly admitted that Rojava is hardly above criticism, but as far as I could see, Rojava at the very least aspires to model tolerance and pluralism in a part of the world that has seen far too much fanaticism and repression—and to whatever extent it succeeds, it deserves commendation.

Rojava's economic model "is the same as its political model," an economics adviser in Derik told us: to create a "community economy," building cooperatives in all sectors and educating the people in the idea. The adviser expressed satisfaction that even though 70 percent of Rojava's resources must go to the war effort, the economy still manages to meet everyone's basic needs.

They strive for self-sufficiency, because they must: the crucial fact is that Rojava exists under an embargo. It can neither export to nor import from its immediate neighbor to the north, Turkey, which would like to see the whole Kurdish project disappear.

Even the KRG, under control of their ethnic kin but economically beholden to Turkey, observes the embargo, although more cross-border KRG-Rojava trade is occurring now in the wake of political developments. But the country still lacks resources. That does not dampen their spirit: "If there is only bread, then we all have a share," the adviser told us.

We visited an economics academy and economic cooperatives: a sewing cooperative in Derik, making uniforms for the defense forces; a cooperative greenhouse, growing cucumbers and tomatoes; a dairy cooperative in Rimelan, where a new shed was under construction.

The Kurdish areas are the most fertile parts of Syria, home to its abundant wheat supply, but the Ba'ath regime had deliberately refrained from industrializing the area, a source of raw materials. Hence wheat was cultivated but could not be milled into flour. We visited a mill, newly constructed since the revolution, improvised from local materials. It now provides flour for the bread consumed in Cizîrê, whose residents get three loaves a day.

Similarly, Cizîrê was Syria's major source of petroleum, with several thousand oil rigs, mostly in the Rimelan area. But the Ba'ath regime ensured that Rojava had no refineries, forcing the oil to be transported to refineries elsewhere in Syria. But since the revolution, Rojavans have improvised two new oil refineries, which are used mainly to provide diesel for the generators that power the canton. The local oil industry, if such it can be called, produces only enough for local needs, nothing more.

A DIY Revolution

The level of improvisation was striking throughout the canton. The more we traveled through Rojava, the more I marveled at the do-it-yourself nature of the revolution, its reliance on local ingenuity and the scarce materials at hand. But it was not until we visited the various academies—the women's academy in

Rimelan and the Mesopotamian Academy in Qamishlo—that I realized that it is integral to the system as a whole.

The education system in Rojava is non-traditional, rejecting ideas of hierarchy, power, and hegemony. Instead of following a teacher-student hierarchy, students teach each other and learn from each other's experience. Students learn what is useful, in practical matters; they "search for meaning," as we were told, in intellectual matters. They do not memorize; they learn to think for themselves and make decisions, to become the subjects of their own lives. They learn to be empowered and to participate in Democratic Autonomy.

Images of Abdullah Öcalan are everywhere, which to Western eyes might suggest something Orwellian: indoctrination, knee-jerk belief. But to interpret those images that way would be to miss the situation entirely. "No one will give you your rights," someone quoted Öcalan to us, "you will have to struggle to obtain them."

And to carry out that struggle, Rojavans know they must educate both themselves and society. Öcalan taught them Democratic Confederalism as a set of principles. Their role has been to figure out how to implement it, in Democratic Autonomy, and thereby to empower themselves.

The Kurds have historically had few friends. They were ignored by the Treaty of Lausanne that divided up the Middle East after World War I. For most of the past century, they suffered as minorities in Turkey, Syria, Iran and Iraq. Their language and culture have been suppressed, their identities denied, their human rights overruled.

They are on the wrong side of NATO, where Turkey is permitted to call the shots on Kurdish matters. They have long been outsiders. That experience has been brutal, involving torture, exile, and war. But it has also given them strength and independence of mind. Öcalan taught them how to reset the terms of their existence in a way that gave them dignity and self-respect.

This do-it-yourself revolution by an educated populace is embargoed by their neighbors and gets along by the skin of its teeth. It is nonetheless an endeavor that pushes the human prospect forward. In the wake of the twentieth century, many people have come to the worst conclusions about human nature, but in the twenty-first, Rojavans are setting a new standard for what human beings are capable of. In a world fast losing hope, they shine as a beacon.

Anyone with a bit of faith in humanity should wish the Rojavans well with their revolution and do what they can to help it succeed. They should demand that their governments stop allowing Turkey to define a rejectionist international policy toward the Kurds and toward Democratic Autonomy. They should demand an end to the embargo against Rojava.

The members of the delegation in which I participated (even though I am not an academic) did their work well. Sympathetic to the revolution, they nonetheless asked challenging questions, about Rojava's economic outlook, about the handling of ethnicity and nationalism, and more. The Rojavans we met, accustomed to grappling with hard questions, responded thoughtfully and even welcomed critique. Readers interested in learning more about the Rojava Revolution may look forward to forthcoming writings by the other delegation members: Welat (Oktay) Ay, Rebecca Coles, Antonia Davidovic, Eirik Eiglad, David Graeber, Thomas Jeffrey Miley, Johanna Riha, Nazan Üstündag, and Christian Zimmer.

As for me, I have much more to say than this short article allows and plan to write a further work, one that incorporates drawings I made during the trip.

Janet Biehl is an independent writer, artist, and translator living in Burlington, Vt. She previously edited The Murray Bookchin Reader and is the author of Ecology or Catastrophe: The Life of Murray Bookchin, forthcoming from Oxford University Press.

The following is a report by an anonymous member of the Turkish/Swiss anarchist non-organization *Karakök Autonome* (The Turksih word *Karakök* translates to "black root.")

The Travel Account of a Karakök Autonome Activist

I HAVE MADE IT TO SURUÇ, A CITY IN TURKEY THAT FORMS PART of the border with Syria. The war is everpresent. And the Turikish military is, too, with its armor and water cannons. The population in the smaller town where I am currently staying swings from a few hundred to several thousand the next day and then back again; many are fleeing from here, but many are also arriving, wanting to get over the border to join the resistance in Kobanê, to fight in the ranks of the YPG/YPJ, to deliver food, hustling up whatever way they can think of to help.

Constant fluctuation is the rule. Over and over again, the Turkish military goes on the attack, using water cannons and teargas to drive people away from the border. Turkey is trying its best to impede any support from reaching Kurdish fighters.

Hundreds of thousands of people have already fled from Kobanê into Turkey. People in Suruç have opened their homes to the refugees. Anywhere from several dozen to several hundred people live provisionally in every available structure. Despite lack of the barest necessities, life goes on. Discussions last all day; information about developments in Kobanê gets passed along; the situation changes minute to minute. Nobody has any idea what could happen before sunup, or what tomorrow will bring.

In spite of everything, there is much laughter. Interaction among people is tender; everyone looks after each other; everyone helps everyone else; no one is left alone. What little there is, is shared.

I heard that yesterday ISIS reached the city center of Kobanê through the sewer system. The YPG was able to fight off the incursion, however, and ISIS fighters retreated back into the sewers, where they were then bombed overnight by the US and France.

Every day between four and five in the afternoon, fighting between the YPG and ISIS begins. Overnight the bombs of the Americans and others are making up the "alliance against ISIS" rain down. During the day, US aircraft circle the city. Because the region is relatively flat, I can hear and see the aircraft, the bombs, the smoke, everything, from here. The events are only a few hundred yards away.

I can also see the low hill that last week fell into the hands of ISIS. It is a location of special strategic importance because the entire city of Kobanê can be observed from there. Last week there were pictures in the media of ISIS flags raised there. Since then, though, the hill could be retaken and is now back in the hands of the YPG. Still, it is presently empty of people—this because at only one hundred yards' remove stands another hill which is occupied by the Turkish military.

I speak with people from Kobanê who have fled here to Suruç. They tell me about the citizens' assemblies, the self-governing structures. Before I came, wasn't sure if the reports I had read and heard were true. Could it be that these tales of Rojava, the liberated region, were embellished? Will I hear from fleeing former Rojava residents that the self-governing structures don't really have much bearing on day-to-day life but operate rather on the fringes while familiar party structures make up the actual government?

But when I speak with residents here, I find that my doubts are unfounded. On the contrary: I am gaining higher esteem for the developments here, as I hear firsthand reports from youths, women, and elderly gentlemen. They describe the citizens' assemblies, how everything is discussed and decided collectively, that everything is managed "from below." They tell me about the women's committees, the communes.

What most astonishes me is that to the citizens of Rojava, these structures are not as big a deal as they often are to us hundreds of miles away. For them it is everyday life. They do not speak of "revolution," but rather talk about something that is, for them, obvious and mundane. There is nothing special about it.

An older woman tells me about the structures in Rojava and paints a picture of a real-existing libertarian society, without using any theoretical terminology or throwing around the names of whatever libertarian gurus. Presumably she doesn't know them, and that doesn't matter in the slightest. Terms and names are superfluous, when there is reality.

I also notice, however, that some are very conscious in their stand for the structures and principles of Rojava. Some also find the whole thing to be anything but wonderful. One citizen fleeing from Kobanê told me that she wishes a state would be established in Rojava. When I asked her why, she said, "then we wouldn't have to do everything ourselves. Politicians can decide and organize the basics."

She is convinced that a state would protect the population. "If we had a state, we wouldn't be getting attacked from all sides. Or at least we would have support from other states." She then relates that she had to give up ninety percent of her land's yield to regions with no agriculture, because it was decided in the citizens' assembly that goods should be as evenly distributed as possible to meet the needs of all; there should not be abundance in one place when there is shortage in another. The woman I spoke to would rather keep her entire yield, or at least a greater portion of it.

I see how alive the revolution in Rojava is, and also the discrepancies that come with it. Under a dictatorship, everyone is supposed to think alike. Here there are varied perspectives— that are also communicated freely and openly.

I heard about a survey that was conducted in Rojava by the committee for research and statistics. The goal was to suss out which political system the citizens of Rojava wanted. Almost 70% stood behind the idea of democratic federalism. Around 30% wanted something else, for instance an Islamic or a national state, or a capitalist system.

Against all odds, the region has maintained this form for over a year now, and proves much stronger than anyone expected.

When ISIS marched on Kobanê, everyone assumed that the city would succumb in a few days. But the population is resisting. Everyone has armed themselves, everyone does guard duty. And now ISIS is retreating; more and more parts of Kobanê are being retaken.

We close this book on a happy note, with an essay written by Dilar Dirik on January 27, 2015, just as the YPG and YPJ have successfully cleared the city of Kobanî of ISIS forces.

Why Kobanî Did Not Fall

ONE YEAR AGO, TODAY, KOBANÎ DECLARED ITSELF AS AN AU-tonomous canton.

Today, after 135 days of fearless resistance, the people of Kobanî have liberated the city from the so-called Islamic State. Since September 2014, the YPG and YPJ have been leading a –there are no other words to describe it- epic and unbelievable resistance against the latest wave of attacks by ISIS. The women and men, who lead the most glorious resistance of our time, hoisted their flags on the last hills that were occupied by ISIS and immediately began their line dances, accompanied by old Kurdish revolutionary songs and slogans. Ever since, people around the world rushed to the streets to celebrate. After the countless tragedies, massacres, and traumas that this region has had to suffer recently, the pains that have preceded this moment make victory even sweeter. One eye sheds tears for the dead, while the other cries out of much deserved joy.

But let us go back one year. It was around this time in January 2014 when major international actors met at the so-called Geneva-II conference to discuss a resolution to the war in Syria. The Kurds, who had been fighting both the regime as well as extremists like the al-Nusra Front and ISIS ever since they [the Kurds] took control over Rojava in 2012, were not invited. Further, in order to pacify the Turkish state, the international community adopted an explicitly hostile attitude towards Rojava, because the main actors in the region are ideologically affiliated with the Kurdistan Workers Party (PKK), the Turkish state's archenemy, which is labeled as "terrorist" by the US, the EU, and Turkey. In fact, the international community marginalised Rojava long before it marginalised the jihadists in Syria. Turkish state officials repeatedly emphasized that they would "not tolerate terrorists by the Syrian-Turkish border," referring to the Kurds in Rojava, not to radical Islamists.

Yet, without relying on anyone's approval, and in spite of all this hostility, the people of Rojava declared three autonomous cantons at the same time as the Geneva-II conference: Kobanî, Afrîn, and Cizîre. The message was: "We will build our autonomy and we do not need anyone's approval."

For the last three years, the Kurds, who took a "third way" and refused to pick either the opposition or Assad, tried to warn the world about ISIS, but were completely ignored. The co-chair of the PYD in Rojava, Salih Muslim, was denied visas to the US four times. In 2013, almost a year before the world even knew about the jihadist group, his son died fighting against ISIS.

The latest wave of attacks on Kobanî is just one out of many that preceded it. All of the Kurd's warnings were discarded as conspiracy theories, simply because listening to them would mean to acknowledge that the anti-Assad bloc has indirectly or directly supported and sponsored jihadist murderers in Syria.

Today, US vice president Joe Biden and others state exactly what the Kurds have been saying for years: states like Saudi Arabia, Qatar, and Turkey supported jihadists. Literally overnight, after thousands of people had been murdered already, ISIS became an "issue," around the same time in which ISIS crossed over into Iraq—the failed state into which the US poured billions of dollars after invading and where many forces hold strategic economic and political interests. And then the same states that formerly supported the jihadists suddenly became part of the coalition against them, including Qatar and Saudi Arabia. After the people in Kobanî had already resisted for more than a month all by themselves, the coalition saw an opportunity to show that their strategy against ISIS works. They suddenly supported the same people they had previously marginalised. But even today, though everyone appropriates Kobanî's resistance for their own agendas, the same forces that lead this resistance are labeled as "terrorist," while there are no consequences for the states that explicitly contributed to the rise of ISIS.

If we lived in a world in which the dominant forces that portray themselves as the defenders of human rights, freedom, and democracy were actually genuinely interested in the principles that they advocate, all of this hell on earth would have been avoided. But leaving aside the fact that arms trade and the destabilisation of the region are profitable for many global actors, another ugly truth is that those who wanted to topple Assad benefitted from jihadist presence in Syria for a long time. This was much to the benefit of the Assad-regime, which kept on claiming that no genuine opposition in Syria exists. And today, the horrid reality is that Assad looks like the lesser evil so that even the coalition seems to soften on him. What a kafkaesque tragedy for the people of Syria!

Considering all of this, are we really expected to congratulate the main instigators of war and conflict in the Middle East for liberating Kobanî?

Those who funded or at least turned a blind eye to murderous jihadists?

Those who started unjust wars and destroyed the region with their policies? Those who appeased the Turkish state, which has supported extremist rapists and murderers?

What is really behind Kobanî's resilience? What does Kobanî symbolize in an era of failed revolutions and endless wars?

The people who are fighting in Kobanî have an ideology, a world view, a vision that has kept them going. Can we say that the coalition air strikes did not help at all? Of course we cannot. But let us ask ourselves why the coalition went from "Kobanî is about to fall and it is not our priority to save it" to putting all efforts into protecting it. Had it not been for the resilience of the people on the ground, who collectively mobilized with Kalashnikovs only to defend their city, the opportunity for the coalition to "rescue" Kobanî for its own interests would not have arisen. After all, half a year before US-led air strikes bombarded ISIS positions around Kobanî, elderly women in their 60s had established their autonomous "mother's" self-defense battalions on the ground. Without these people's determination and willingness to sacrifice, no air strikes on earth would have saved the city.

It is important to understand that the Rojava revolution has been a people's struggle from the beginning until today. Unlike other uprisings in the recent times, it was luckily not co-opted by anyone due to geopolitical conditions and survived by relying on its own strength, against all odds. Kobanî's courageous stance against the men who want to draw the colors of the Middle East black resonated with struggling people all over the world. Many are praising and some are instrumentalising Kobanî now, even right-wingers and Islamophobes, because everyone wants a piece of the victory pie. But the same powers that now appropriate Kobanî for their own interests label the politics of these courageous fighters as terrorist. The resistance of Kobanî is based on a rooted tradition and did not appear out of nowhere. The fighters emphasize that it is the philosophy of the PKK that motivates their struggle. When liberating Kobanî, the fighters immediately chanted "Bijî Serok Apo"—Long live Apo (Abdullah Öcalan, the PKK's imprisoned ideological representative).

In other words, the strongest enemies of ISIS are internationally labeled as terrorist, just like the rapist, fascist jihadist murderers. Similarly, everyone is trying to instrumentalise the suffering of the Yazidi people from Mount Sinjar (Shengal) for their own interests, but the thousands of Yazidi refugees in the Rojava state that the international community is doing nothing for them, while it was the YPG/YPJ and PKK that have rescued them in August and looked after them ever since, in spite of the embargo on Rojava and the war in Kobanî.

Uncomfortable facts for those who portray themselves as the rescuers!

Rojava is an alternative for the region, torn by ethnic and religious hatred, unjust wars, and economic exploitation. It does not aim to build a new state, but to create an alternative system to the global capitalist, male-dominated nation-state paradigm by advocating regional autonomy through women's liberation and in cooperation with all peoples of the region, termed as "Democratic Confederalism" by Öcalan.

The refusal to accept the parameters of the global system is what has mobilised the population in such a devastated region, in between war and embargo, and this is precisely the reason why Kobanî will never fall. In the midst of war, Rojava's cantons have managed to establish an incredibly empowering women's movement, a self-governance system that operates through local councils in a bottom-up grassroots fashion, and a society in which all ethnic and religious components of the region work hand-in-hand to create a brighter future. This is in radical contrast to the monopolist "one religion, one language, one nation, one state, one flag" policies, the dictatorships, monarchies, sectarian tyrannies, and patriarchal violence in the region. And the anticipation of such a free life is the main motor of the Kobanî resistance. The dominant system makes us believe that principles and ideals are dead, which is why a collective mobilisation and sacrificial resistance such as the one in Kobanî seems so unbelievable to most people. But the fact that the second largest city of Iraq, Mosul, fell into ISIS's hands within days, even though the US had put billions of dollars into training the Iraqi army, while the small city of Kobanî, where elderly women created their autonomous battalions, has become a fortress of resistance for people across the globe, shows us that the possibility of a different future is well alive!

You cannot separate the political mobilisation of the people in Rojava from their victories against ISIS. That is why the least we can do to honor the fighters of Kobanî is to respect and support their political aims! The recognition of the Rojava cantons is long overdue. But even if the world does not recognise Rojava, it will still insist on being, because it has proven that it does not need anyone's approval to exist. It is exactly this resistance, will, and self-reliant struggle, this refusal to subscribe to the Stockholm-symptom-like state in which the Middle East finds itself, so much that it is forced to be happy over "democracy" that comes in forms of breadcrumbs, that has not allowed Kobanî to fall.

The victory and dignity of Kobanî should give hope to all peoples of the Middle East and beyond. Surrounded by the dark flag of ISIS, the bloodthirsty Assad-regime, the vicious Turkish state, a suffocating embargo, cold-blooded foreign policy calculations by global hegemonic powers, ethnic tensions, and sectarian wars, the smiling people of Kobanî have stuck to their liberationist revolutionary principles and helped the sun of Mesopotamia rise against all of this darkness.

Victory belongs to those who dedicated their lives to it. Let us honor the braveness of these selfless human beings and the victims of the war by exposing the policies and interests of the states and structures that created this inferno to begin with.

May we look forward to more revolutionary moments of joy like today and never forget those, who dedicated their lives to it!

Bijî Kobanî!

Appendix A

The Constitution of the Rojava Cantons

The Social Contract of Rojava Cantons in Syria

Preamble

We, the people of the Democratic Autonomous Regions of Afrin, Cizîrê and Kobanî, a confederation of Kurds, Arabs, Syrics, Arameans, Turkmen, Armenians and Chechens, freely and solemnly declare and establish this Charter.

In pursuit of freedom, justice, dignity and democracy and led by principles of equality and environmental sustainability, the Charter proclaims a new social contract, based upon mutual and peaceful coexistence and understanding between all strands of society. It protects fundamental human rights and liberties and reaffirms the peoples' right to self-determination.

Under the Charter, we, the people of the Autonomous Regions, unite in the spirit of reconciliation, pluralism and democratic participation so that all may express themselves freely in public life. In building a society free from authoritarianism, militarism, centralism and the intervention of religious authority in public affairs, the Charter recognizes Syria's territorial integrity and aspires to maintain domestic and international peace.

In establishing this Charter, we declare a political system and civil administration founded upon a social contract that reconciles the rich mosaic of Syria through a transitional phase from dictatorship, civil war and destruction, to a new democratic society where civic life and social justice are preserved.

I. General Principles

Article 1

The Charter of the Autonomous Regions of Afrin, Cizîrê, and Kobanî, [hereinafter "the Charter"], is a renewed social contract between the peoples of the Autonomous Regions. The Preamble is an integral part of the Charter.

Article 2

a) Authority resides with and emanates from the people of the Autonomous Regions. It is exercised by governing councils and public institutions elected by popular vote.

b) The people constitute the sole source of legitimacy all governing councils and public institutions, which are founded on democratic principles essential to a free society.

Article 3

a) Syria is a free, sovereign and democratic state, governed by a parliamentary system based on principles of decentralization and pluralism.

b) The Autonomous Regions is composed of the three cantons of Afrin, Cizîrê and Kobanî, forming an integral part of the Syrian territory. The administrative centers of each canton are: Afrin city, canton of Afrin; Qamishli city, canton of Cizîrê; Kobanî city, canton of Kobanî.

c) The canton of Cizîrê is ethnically and religiously diverse, with Kurdish, Arab, Syriac, Chechen, Armenian, Muslim, Christian and Yazidi communities peacefully co-existing in brotherhood. The elected Legislative Assembly represents all three cantons of the Autonomous Regions.

The Structure of Governance in the Autonomous Regions

Article 4

1) Legislative Assembly

2) Executive Councils

3) High Commission of Elections

4) Supreme Constitutional Courts

5) Municipal/Provincial Councils

Article 5

The administrative centers of each canton are:

Qamishli city, canton of Cizîrê;

Afrin city, canton of Afrin;

Kobanî City, canton of Kobanî.

Article 6

All persons and communities are equal in the eyes of the law and in rights and responsibilities.

Article 7

All cities, towns and villages in Syria which accede to this Charter may form cantons falling within Autonomous Regions.

Article 8

All cantons in the Autonomous Regions are founded upon the principle of local self-government. Cantons may freely elect their representatives and representative bodies, and may pursue their rights insofar as it does not contravene the articles of the Charter.

Article 9

The official languages of the canton of Cizîrê are Kurdish, Arabic and Syriac. All communities have the right to teach and be taught in their native language.

Article 10

The Autonomous Regions shall not interfere in the domestic affairs of other countries, and it shall safeguard its relations with neighboring states, resolving any conflicts peacefully.

Article 11

The Autonomous Regions have the right to be represented by their own flag, emblems and anthem. Such symbols shall be defined in a law.

Article 12

The Autonomous Regions form an integral part of Syria. It is a model for a future decentralized system of federal governance in Syria.

II. Basic Principles

Article 13

There shall be a separation of powers between the legislature, executive and judiciary.

Article 14

The Autonomous Regions shall seek to implement a framework of transitional justice measures. It shall take steps to redress the legacy of chauvinistic and discriminatory State policies, including the payment of reparations to victims, both individuals and communities, in the Autonomous Regions.

Article 15

The People's Protection Units (YPG) is the sole military force of the three cantons, with the mandate to protect and defend the security of the Autonomous Regions and its peoples, against both internal and external threats. The People's

Protection Units act in accordance with the recognized inherent right to self-defense. Power of command in respect of the People's Protection Units is vested in the Body of Defense through its Central Command. Its relation to the armed forces of the central Government shall be defined by the Legislative Assembly in a special law.

The Asayish forces are charged with civil policing functions in the Autonomous Regions.

Article 16

If a court or any other public body considers that a provision conflicts with a provision of a fundamental law or with a provision of any other superior statute, or that the procedure prescribed was set aside in any important respect when the provision was introduced, the provision shall be nullified.

Article 17

The Charter guarantees the rights of the youth to participate actively in public and political life.

Article 18

Unlawful acts and omissions and the appropriate penalties are defined by criminal and civil law.

Article 19

The system of taxation and other fiscal regulations are defined by law.

Article 20

The Charter holds as inviolable the fundamental rights and freedoms set out in international human rights treaties, conventions and declarations.

III. Rights and Liberties

Article 21

The Charter incorporates the Universal Declaration of Human Rights, the International Covenant on Civil and Political Rights, the International Covenant on Economic, Social and Cultural Rights, as well as other internationally recognized human rights conventions.

Article 22

All international rights and responsibilities pertaining civil, political, cultural, social and economical rights are guaranteed.

Article 23

a) Everyone has the right to express their ethnic, cultural, linguistic and gender rights
b) Everyone has the right to live in a healthy environment, based on ecology balance.

Article 24

Everyone has the right to freedom of opinion and expression; including freedom to hold opinions without interference and to seek, receive and impart information and ideas through any media and regardless of frontiers.

Freedom of expression and freedom of information may be restricted having regard to the security of the Autonomous Regions, public safety and order, the integrity of the individual, the sanctity of private life, or the prevention and prosecution of crime.

Article 25

a) Everyone has the right to liberty and security of person.

b) All persons deprived of their liberty shall be treated with humanity and with respect for the inherent dignity of the human person. No one shall be subjected to torture or to cruel, inhuman or degrading treatment or punishment.

c) Prisoners have the right to humane conditions of detention, which protect their inherent dignity. Prisons shall serve the underlying objective of the reformation, education and social rehabilitation of prisoners.

Article 26

Every human being has the inherent right to life. No one within the jurisdiction of the Autonomous Regions shall be executed.

Article 27

Women have the inviolable right to participate in political, social, economic and cultural life.

Article 28

Men and women are equal in the eyes of the law. The Charter guarantees the effective realization of equality of women and mandates public institutions to work towards the elimination of gender discrimination.

Article 29

The Charter guarantees the rights of the child. In particular children shall not suffer economic exploitation, child labor, torture or cruel, inhuman or degrading treatment or punishment, and shall not be married before attaining the age of majority.

Article 30

All persons have the right
1) to personal security in a peaceful and stable society.
2) to free and compulsory primary and secondary education.
3) to work, social security, health, adequate housing.
4) to protect the motherhood and maternal and pediatric care.
5) to adequate health and social care for the disabled, the elderly and those with special needs.

Article 31

Everyone has the right to freedom of worship, to practice one's own religion either individually or in association with others. No one shall be subjected to persecution on the grounds of their religious beliefs.

Article 32

a) Everyone has the right to freedom of association with others, including the right to establish and freely join any political party, association, trade union and/or civil assembly.
b) In exercising the right to freedom of association, political, economic and cultural expression of all communities is

protected. This serves to protect the rich and diverse heritage of the peoples of the Autonomous Regions.

c) The Yazidi religion is a recognized religion and its adherents' rights to freedom of association and expression is explicitly protected. The protection of Yazidi religious, social and cultural life may be guaranteed through the passage of laws by the Legislative Assembly.

Article 33

Everyone has the freedom to obtain, receive and circulate information and to communicate ideas, opinions and emotions, whether orally, in writing, in pictorial representations, or in any other way.

Article 34

Everyone has the right of peaceful assembly, including the right to peaceful protect, demonstration and strike.

Article 35

Everyone has the right to freely experience and contribute to academic, scientific, artistic and cultural expressions and creations, through individual or joint practice, to have access to and enjoy, and to disseminate their expressions and creations.

Article 36

Everyone has the right to vote and to run for public office, as circumscribed by law.

Article 37

Everyone has the right to seek political asylum. Persons may only be deported following a decision of a competent, impartial and properly constituted judicial body, where all due process rights have been afforded.

Article 38

All persons are equal before the law and are entitled to equal opportunities in public and professional life.

Article 39

Natural resources, located both above and below ground, are the public wealth of society. Extractive processes, management, licensing and other contractual agreements related to such resources shall be regulated by law.

Article 40

All buildings and land in the Autonomous Regions are owned by the Transitional Administration are public property. The use and distribution shall be determined by law.

Article 41

Everyone has the right to the use and enjoyment of his private property. No one shall be deprived of his property except upon payment of just compensation, for reasons of public utility or social interest, and in the cases and according to the forms established by law.

Article 42

The economic system in the provinces shall be directed at providing general welfare and in particular granting funding to science and technology. It shall be aimed at guaranteeing the daily needs of people and to ensure a dignified life. Monopoly is prohibited by law. Labor rights and sustainable development are guaranteed.

Article 43

Everyone has the right to liberty of movement and freedom to choose his residence within the Autonomous Regions.

Article 44

The enumeration of the rights and freedoms set forth in Section III is non-exhaustive.

The Democratic Self-rule Administration Project

IV. Legislative Assembly

Article 45

The Legislative Assembly in the Autonomous Region is elected by the people by direct, secret ballot, and the duration of the course is four (4) years.

Article 46

The first meeting of the Legislative Assembly shall be held no later than the 16th day following the announcement of the final results of elections in all Autonomous Regions. Such results will be certified and announced by the Higher Commission of Elections.

The President of the Transitional Executive Council will convene the first meeting of the Legislative Assembly. If compelling reasons dictate that its first meeting cannot be so held, the President of the Transitional Executive Council will determine another date to be held within fifteen days.

Quorum is met by fifty + one (50+1%) percent attendants of the total. The oldest member of the Legislative Assembly will chair its first meeting at which the Co-Presidents and Executive Council will be elected.

The sessions of the Legislative Assembly are public unless necessity demands otherwise. The movement of the Legislative Assembly into closed session is governed by its rules of procedure.

Article 47

There shall be one member of the Supreme Legislature Council per fifteen thousand (15,000) registered voters residing within the Autonomous Region. The Legislative Assembly must be composed of at least forty per cent (40%) of either sex according to the electoral laws. The representation of the Syriac community, as well as youth representation in the election lists, is governed by electoral laws.

Article 48

1) No member of the Legislative Assembly may run for more than two consecutive terms.

2) The term of the Legislative Assembly may be extended in exceptional cases at the request of one quarter (¼) of its members or at the request of the Office of the President of the Council, with the consent of two-thirds (⅔) of the members of the Council. Such extension shall be for no longer than six (6) months.

Article 49

Every person who has reached the age of eighteen (18) years is eligible to vote. Candidates for the Legislative Assembly must have attained the age of twenty-two (22) years. Conditions for candidacy and election are stipulated by electoral law.

Article 50

Members of the Legislative Assembly enjoy immunity in respect of acts and omissions carried out in the function of official duties. Any prosecutions require the authorization of the Legislative Assembly, with the exception of flagrante crime. At the earliest opportunity, the Office of the President of the Council shall be informed of all pending prosecutions.

Article 51

No member, during his term of office, is permitted any public, private, or other profession. Such employment is suspended once he makes the constitutional oath. He has the right to return to his job, with all its rights and benefits, once his membership ends.

Article 52
Local Councils in each province of the Autonomous Regional shall be formed through direct elections.

Article 53
The functions of the Legislative Assembly are to:
- Establish rules and procedures governing the work of the Legislative Assembly.
- Enact legislation and proposed regulations for the Local Councils and other institutions, including permanent and ad hoc committees, under its purview.
- Exercise control over administrative and executive bodies, including use of powers of review.
- Ratification of international treaties and agreements.
- Delegate its powers to the Executive Council or to one of its members and thereafter to withdraw such powers.
- Declare a State of war and peace.
- Ratify the appointment of members of the Supreme Constitutional Court.
- Adopt the general budget.
- Establish general policy and development plans.
- Approve and grant amnesty.
- Adopt decrees promulgated by the Executive Council; and
- Adopt laws for the common governance of the Provincial Councils of the Autonomous Regions.

V. Executive Council

Article 54
Canton Premier

A) The Canton Premier, together with the Executive Council of the Autonomous Regions, hold executive authority as set forth in this Charter.

B) The candidate to the post of Canton Premier must.

1) Be over thirty-five years of age;
2) Be a Syrian citizen and a resident of the canton; and
3) Have no convictions or cautions.

C) The procedure governing the candidacy and election of Canton Premier:

1) Within 30 days of the first session of the Legislative Assembly, its President must call for the election of the Canton Premiers.
2) Requests to nominate candidates for the position of Canton Premier must be made, in writing, to the Supreme Court which shall examine and accept or reject not later than ten (10) days after the close of nominations.
3) The Legislative Assembly shall elect the Canton Premier by a simple majority.
4) If no candidate receives the required simple majority, a second electoral round is initiated, with the candidate receiving the highest number of votes, being elected.
5) The term of Canton Premier is four (4) years from the date of the taking of the Oath of Office;
6) The Canton Premier makes the Oath of Office before the Legislative Assembly before commencing official duties.
7) The Canton Premier appointed one or more Deputies,

approved by the Legislative Assembly. The Deputies take an Oath of Office before the Canton Premier, after which specified functions may be delegated to them.

8) Should the Canton Premier be unable to fulfill his official functions, one of his Deputies shall replace him. Where the Canton Premier and the Deputies are unable to fulfill their duties for any reason, the tasks of the Canton Premier will be carried out by the President of the Legislative Assembly; and

9) The Governor must address any letter of resignation to the Legislative Assembly.

D) The powers and functions of the Canton Premier:

1) The Canton Premier shall ensure respect for the Charter and the protection of the national unity and sovereignty, and at all times performing his functions to the best of ability and conscience.

2) The Canton Premier shall appoint the President of the Executive Council.

3) The Canton Premier shall implement laws passed by the Legislative Assembly, and issue decisions, orders and decrees in accordance with those laws.

4) The Canton Premier must invite the newly elected Legislative Assembly to convene within fifteen (15) days from the announcement of the election results;

5) The Canton Premier may grant medals.

6) The Canton Premier may issue amnesties as recommended by the President of the Executive Council.

E) The Canton Premier is responsible to the people through his representatives in the Legislative Assembly. The Legislative Assembly has the right to bring him before the Supreme

Constitutional Court for charges of treason and other forms of sedition.

The Executive Council:

The Executive Council is the highest executive and administrative body in the Autonomous Regions. It is responsible for the implementation of laws, resolutions and decrees as issued by the Legislative Assembly and judicial institutions. It shall coordinate the institutions of the Autonomous Regions.

Article 55

The Executive Council is composed of a Chairman, representatives and committees.

Article 56

The party or bloc winning a majority of seats in the Legislative Assembly shall form the Executive Council within one month from the date of assignment, with the approval of the simple majority (51%) of the members of the Legislative Assembly.

Article 57

The Head of the Executive Council shall not serve more than two consecutive terms, each term being four (4) years in length. Article 58 The Head of the Executive Council may choose advisers amongst the newly elected members of the Legislative Council.

Article 59
Each adviser shall be responsible for one of the bodies within the Executive Council.

Article 60
The work of the Executive Council, including the Departments, and their relation to other institutions/committees is regulated by law.

Article 61
After the formation and approval of the Executive Council, it shall issue its prospective Program for Government. Following its passage through the Legislative Assembly, the Executive Council is obliged to implement the Program of Government during that legislative term.

Article 62
Senior civil servants and Department representatives shall be nominated by the Executive Council and approved by the Legislative Council.

Provincial Administrative Councils [Municipal Councils]:

1) The cantons of the Autonomous Regions are composed of Provincial Administrative Councils [Municipal Councils] and are managed by the relevant Executive Council which retains the power to amend its functions and regulations;

2) The powers and duties of the Provincial Administrative Councils [Municipal Councils] are founded upon an adherence to a policy of decentralization. The canton's supervision

of the Provincial Administrative Councils' [Municipal Councils'] authority, including its budget and finance, public services and mayoral elections are regulated by law.

3) Provincial Administrative Councils [Municipal Councils] are directly elected by the public, using secret ballot.

VI. The Judicial Council

Article 63

The independence of the Judiciary is founding principle of the rule of law, which ensures a just and effective disposition of cases by the competent and impartial courts.

Article 64

Everyone charged with a criminal offence shall be presumed innocent until and unless proved guilty by a competent and impartial court.

Article 65

All institutions of the Judicial Council must be composed of at least forty per cent (40%) of either sex.

Article 66

The right to defense is sacred and inviolable at all stages of an investigation and trial.

Article 67

The removal of a Judge from office requires a decision from the Judicial Council.

Article 68

Judgments and judicial decisions are issued on behalf of the people.

Article 69

Failure to implement judicial decisions and orders is a violation of law.

Article 70

No civilian shall stand trial before any military court or special or ad hoc tribunals.

Article 71

Searches of houses and other private property must be done in accordance with a properly executed warrant, issued by a judicial authority.

Article 72

Everyone is entitled in full equality to a fair and public hearing by an independent and impartial tribunal, in the determination of his rights and obligations and of any criminal charge against him.

Article 73

No one shall be subjected to arbitrary arrest or detention. No one shall be deprived of his liberty except on such grounds and in accordance with such procedure as are established by law.

Article 74

Anyone who has been the victim of unlawful arrest or detention or otherwise suffered damage or harm as a result of the acts and omissions of public authorities has an enforceable right to compensation.

Article 75

The Judicial Council is established by law.

VII.
The Higher Commission of Elections

Article 76

The Higher Commission of Elections is an independent body competent to oversee and run the electoral process. It is composed of 18 members, representing all cantons, who are appointed by the Legislative Assembly.

1) Decisions in the Commission require a qualified majority of eleven (11) votes.

2) Member of the Higher Commission of Elections may not stand for office in the Legislative Assembly.

3) The Higher Commission of Elections determines the date on which elections are held, the announcement of the results, and receive the nominations of eligible candidates for the Legislative Assembly.

4) As stated in paragraph 51, the Higher Commission of Elections verifies the eligibility of candidates seeking election to the Legislative Assembly. The Higher Commission of Elections is the sole body competent to receive allegations of electoral fraud, voter intimidation or illegal interference with the process of an election.

5) The Higher Commission of Elections is monitored by the Supreme Court and may be monitored by observers from the United Nations and civil society organizations.

6) The Higher Commission of Elections, together with the Judicial Council, shall convene a meeting of all candidates seeking election to the Legislative Assembly to announce the names of eligible candidates.

VIII. The Supreme Constitutional Court

Article 77

a) The Supreme Constitutional Court is composed of seven (7) members, all of whom are nominated by the Legislative Assembly. Its members are drawn from Judges, legal experts and lawyers, all of whom must have no less than fifteen (15) years of professional experience.

b) No member of the Supreme Constitutional Court shall not be eligible to serve on the Executive Council or in the Legislative Assembly or to hold any other office or position of emolument, as defined by law.

c) A member's term of office runs for four (4) years. No member may serve more than two terms.

The Functions of the Supreme Constitutional Court:

Article 78

1) To interpret the articles and underlying principles of the Charter.
2) To determine the constitutionality of laws enacted by the Legislative Assembly and decisions taken by Executive Council.
3) To judicially review legislative acts and executive decisions, where such acts and decisions may be in the conflict with the letter and spirit of the Charter and the Constitution.
4) Canton Premiers, members of the Legislative Assembly and Executive Council may be brought before the Supreme Constitutional Court, when alleged to have acted in breach of the Charter.
5) Its decisions are reached through simple majority vote.

Article 79

A member of the Supreme Constitutional Court shall not be removed from office except for stated misbehavior or incapacity. The provisions and procedures governing the work of the Supreme Constitutional Court shall be set out in a special law.

Article 80

Procedure for determination of the constitutionality of laws as follow:

1) The decision for the non-constitutional of any law will be as follow:

a) Where, prior to a law's enactment, more than twenty per cent (20%) of the Legislative Assembly objects to its constitutionality, the Supreme Constitutional Court is seized of the matter and shall render its decision within fifteen (15) days; if the law is to be urgently enacted, a decision shall be rendered within seven (7) days.

b) Where, following the rendering of the Judgment of the Supreme Constitutional Court, more than twenty per cent (20%) of the Legislative Assembly still objects to its constitutionality, an appeal may be lodged.

c) If, on appeal, the Supreme Constitutional Court rules the law to be enacted as unconstitutional, the law shall be considered null and void.

2. If an argument is raised in a court concerning the constitutionality of a law as follow:

a) If parties to a case raise a challenge to the constitutionality of a law and the court so holds, the matter is stayed while it is referred to the Supreme Constitutional Court

b) The Supreme Constitutional Court must deliver its judgment within thirty (30) days.

IX. General Rules

Article 81

The Charter applies within the Autonomous Regions. It may only be amended by a qualified majority of two-thirds (⅔) of the Legislative Assembly.

Article 82

The Charter shall be laid before the Transitional Legislative Assembly for review and ratification.

Article 83

Syrian citizens holding dual nationality are barred from assuming leading positions in the Office of the Canton Premier, the Provincial Council, and the Supreme Constitutional Court.

Article 84

The Charter sets out the legislative framework through which laws, decrees, and states of emergency shall be formally implemented.

Article 85

Elections to form the Legislative Assembly shall be held within four (4) months of the ratification of the Charter by the Transitional Legislative Assembly. The Transitional Legislative Assembly retains the right to extend the time period if exceptional circumstances arise.

Article 86

The Oath of Office to be taken by members of the Legislative Assembly

"I solemnly swear, in the name of Almighty God, to abide by the Charter and laws of the Autonomous Regions, to defend the liberty and interests of the people, to ensure the security of the Autonomous Regions, to protect the rights of legitimate self-defense and to strive for social justice, in accordance with the principles of democratic rules enshrined herein."

Article 87

All governing bodies, institutions and committees shall be made up of at least forty percent (40%) of either sex.

Article 88

Syrian criminal and civil legislation is applicable in the Autonomous Regions except where it contradicts provisions of this Charter.

Article 89

In the case of conflict between laws passed by the Legislative Assembly and legislation of the central government, the Supreme Constitutional Court will rule upon the applicable law, based on the best interest of the Autonomous Regions.

Article 90

The Charter guarantees the protection of the environment and regards the sustainable development of natural ecosystems as a moral and a sacred national duty.

Article 91

The education system of the Autonomous Regions shall be based upon the values of reconciliation, dignity, and pluralism. It is a marked departure from prior education policies founded upon racist and chauvinistic principles.

Education within the Autonomous Regions rejects prior education policies based on racist and chauvinistic principles. Founded upon the values of reconciliation, dignity, and pluralism,

a) The new educational curriculum of the cantons shall recognize the rich history, culture and heritage of the peoples of the Autonomous Regions.

b) The education system, public service channels and academic institutions shall promote human rights and democracy.

Article 92

a) The Charter enshrines the principle of separation of religion and State.

b) Freedom of religion shall be protected. All religions and faiths in the Autonomous Regions shall be respected. The right to exercise religious beliefs shall be guaranteed, insofar as it does not adversely affect the public good.

Article 93

a) The promotion of cultural, social and economic advancement by administrative institutions ensures enhanced stability and public welfare within the Autonomous Regions.

b) There is no legitimacy for authority which contradicts this charter. Article 94 Martial law may be invoked and revoked by a qualified majority of two-thirds (⅔) of the Executive Council, in a special session chaired by the Canton Premier. The decision must then be presented to and unanimously adopted by the Legislative Assembly, with its provisions contained in a special law.

The Executive Council Bodies

Article 95

1) Body of Foreign Relations

2) Body of Defense

3) Body of Internal Affairs

4) Body of Justice
5) Body of Cantonal and Municipal Councils and affiliated to it Committee of Planning and Census
6) Body of Finance, and affiliated to it
  a) Committee on Banking Regulations.
  b) Committee of Customs and Excise.
7) Body of Social Affairs
8) Body of Education
9) Body of Agriculture
10) Body of Energy.
11) Body of Health
12) Body of Trade and Economic Cooperation
13) Body of Martyrs and Veterans Affairs
14) Body of Culture
15) Body of Transport
16) Body of Youth and Sports
17) Body of Environment, Tourism and Historical Objects
18) Body of Religious Affairs
19) Body of Family and Gender Equality
20) Body of Human Rights.
21) Body of Communications
22) Body of Food

Security Article 96
The Charter shall be published in the media and press.

1847-1880
Kurdish uprisings in Ottoman Empire. 30,000 Kurds died during supression by Ottomans.

1920
Collapse of Ottoman Empire - Treaty of Sèvres promises autonomous state to the Kurds.

1923
Turkey recognized as an independent nation, Treaty of Lausanne replaces Treaty of Sèvres. Kurdish region divided among Turkey, Iraq, and Syria.

1920 -27
Ataturk puts all Kurdish regions in Turkey under martial law, arrests tens of thousands of Kurds, bans the language, opposition press and gatherings of more than 15 people (including funerals and weddings).

1950 - 59
Assimilation policies in Turkey and Syria. Kurdish political parties and organizations recognized.

1961
Civil war in Iraq between Ba'athist government and Kurds in the north.

1916-18
Ethnic cleansing, displacement and starvation by the "Young Turks" of Kurds of Erzurum and Bitlis. 700,000 deported, 35%-50% perish.

1922 -24
Kingdom of Kurdistan in Northern Iraq supported by National Ba'athist Organization

1927
Kurds declare independent Republic of Ararat, supported by the United Kingdom.

1946
Iranian Kurds create the Mahabad Republic with Soviet Support.

1960
Coup d'Etat in Turkey, Kurdish parties along with other liberal political parties outlawed.

Appendix B
a timeline of Kurdish resistance

1975
PUK is formed and starts a long lasting conflict with KDP in Iraq.

1970
Iraq government signs treaties granting Kurds limited autonomy.

1979
PKK starts a "war of liberation" to create a Kurdish state inside Turkey and Northern Syria. Ayatollah Khomeini's revolution in Iran sparks a Kurdish uprising in Northern Iran.

1980 - 88
Iraqi government attacks the Kurds using military, airforce and chemical weapons in the UN describes as genocide.

1988
PKK launches a "Women's Education Project", brings feminist ideas to their Marxism and sets up women battalions.

1968 -71
General strikes, bombing campaigns and civil unrest by both the right and left in Turkey.

1971
Second military Coup to restore order in Turkey and crush the left.

1978
Kurdistan Worker's Party (PKK) founded by Appo who was part of the leftist student protests of the late 1960's and early 70's.

1980
A third coup in Turkey (backed by the US) to restore order as civil conflict rages between the left and the right. Thousands are arrested. Most of the PKK leaders go into hiding or leave Turkey.

1984
PKK becomes a paramilitary organization, carries out attacks in Turkey and Europe.

1989
First PKK Womens' school created with a policy of co-command requiring a woman and a man to command regions, battalions and other organizations inside the PKK, except for the presidency of the PKK.

1990 - 1991
First Gulf War against Iraq

1992
The PUK and KUP set up first government in Iraqi Kurdistan. Turkey wages a military operation against Kurdish safe havens in Iraq.

1993 - 96
Large scale protests in support of the Kurds and PKK appear regularly in Europe and Turkey.

1998
The KDP and PUK sign a peace treaty ending 4 years of hostilities.

1990 - 99
PKK loses support from Syria and the Soviets but continues to carry out attacks in Turkey.

1991
PKK begins a "decentralized strategy", removes most power from the Central Committee. In Iraq, an uprising (backed by the US) pushed out the Iraqi military and government creates a Federal Autonomous region called Kurdistan.

1993
Germany bans the PKK as a terrorist organization.

1995
Syria withdraws support for the PKK and deports all PKK leaders. Turkey leads a massive military operation against Kurd bases in Iraq.

1999
Appo is arrested in Nairobi by Turkish secret police and sentenced to death (later changed to life imprisonment). Second ceasefire between PKK and the Turkish Government.

2002
The EU and the USA designate the PKK a terrprist organization and freeze bank assets. Kurdish Parliament meets for the first time in Iraq.

2004
PKK changes its name to KADEK

2012
Rojava Republic is declared in Northern Syria by the KNC and PYD. The first self defense militias are formed (YPG/YPJ).

April 2014
The Kurdistan Government in Iraq calls for an independence referendum to be held "in the very near future".

September 2014
YPG/YPJ rescue the fleeing Yazidis in Iraq. The US starts air strikes against ISIS in and around Kobane.

2003-11
Iraq War

2005
PKK ends ceasefire.

2013
Syrian government troops and various rebel militias try to occupy the Rojava Republic but are stopped by the YPG/YPJ. Rojava Principles are adopted.

August2014
ISIS begins siege of Kobane, which is being defended by the YPG/YPJ

October 2014
Turkey refuses to support the YPG/YPJ. Anarchists break across the border to join the fighters. Peshmerga are granted limited access through Turkey to support the defenders of Kobane.

Appendix C
A Lexicon

Abdullah Öcalan (AKA Apo): 67-year-old Kurdish founder and president of the PKK. He has been imprisoned by the Turkish government since 1999. He is the current president of the PKK and is its main ideological architect.

AKP: Acronym for *Adalet ve Kalkınma Partisi,* the Justice and Development Party, Turkey's ruling political party. AKP is a socially conservative political party and uses draconian measures like censorship, arrests, and overwhelming force against demonstrations of dissent in Turkey.

al-Nusra Front: This relatively large and organized Syrian militia is a branch of Al Qaeda, started in the summer of 2012.

Al-Anfal Campaign: Genocide committed against the Kurds and other minorities in Iraq between 1986 and 1989 by Iraqi forces loyal to the Ba'athist Party under Saddam Hussein.

Alawite: Shia religious minority found in Lebanon, Turkey, and most prevalently in Syria. Bashar Al-Assad derives much of his support from this ethno-religious group.

Asayish: The Kurdish word for "Security" and the name of the Kurdish community protection forces within the Rojava cantons, also the main police force within the KRG.

Ba'athist Party: Pan-Arab Nationalist movement that later went on to hold power in both Iraq and Syria under different factions. Secular and nominally leftist, but in reality very dictatorial and militaristic, the Ba'athist Party is perhaps most famous for becoming the political party of Saddam Hussein.

BDP: Turkish acronym for *Barış ve Demokrasi Partisi*, the Peace and Democracy Party. BDP is a Turkish political party founded after the Democratic Society Party (DTP) was banned by Turkish courts in 2008 for being a front for the PKK. The BDP is the current political party most sympathetic to Kurdish rights and the PKK in Turkey. There is a currently an investigation by Turkish authorities into this political party.

FSA: Acronym for the Free Syrian Army, which was originally called the Free Officers Movement (FOM). It was started in 2011 by defecting Syrian military officers who refused to attack protestors and "declared war" on any armed force that did. The FSA leadership is made up of mainly Sunni ex-military officers. It welcomes defections from all parts of the Syrian Government's security forces (police and military) and has sought to coordinate the various militia groups in Syria. It currently is estimated to have a force of about 40,000. It supports and is supported by both the SNC and National Coalition for Syrian Revolutionary and Opposition Forces (NCSROF).

HPG: Kurdish acronym for *Hêzên Parastina Gel*, the People's Defense Force. The HPG is technically the official name of the PKK's armed wing but it is often used interchangeably with PKK. In 1992 it was changed to Kurdistan National Liberty Army (ARGK) but most still refer to it by its old name HPG or just PKK.

HRK: Kurdish acronym for *Hêzên Rojhilata Kurdistan*, the East Kurdistan Defense Forces. HRK is the armed wing of the PJAK in Iran. The HRK have carried out ambushes, industrial sabotage, and robberies aimed against the Iranian state since 2005. A few thousand people on both sides of the conflict have died as the result of the fighting.

ISIS: The Islamic State of Iraq and Syria, also known as The Islamic State of Iraq and Al-Sham, The Islamic State of Iraq and The Levant, and more recently The Islamic State (IS). ISIS is hardline conservative Sunni jihadist group formed as a radical offshoot of Al-Qaeda It is incredibly violent, practicing crucifixion and sex slavery. ISIS controls a large swath of territory in Syria and Iraq and declared itself a caliphate with its capital in Ar-Raqqah, Syria.

KADEK: Kurdish acronym for Kurdistan Freedom and Democracy Congress, the name the PKK adopted for itself for awhile in 2002. one of the many names that the PKK.

KCK: Kurdish acronym for *Koma Civakên Kurdistan*, the Group of Communities in Kurdistan. An umbrella organization, started by the PKK in 2007 to replace the KKK (*Koma Komalên Kurdistan)* to put in practice the ideas of Democratic Confederalism. It is an international group and covers Kurdish groups in Turkey, Syria, Iran, Iraq, and ex-USSR regions. Most of the KCK's activities have been in southern Turkey.

KNC: Acronym for the Kurdish National Congress in Syria. The KNC is a political coalition that came about as a result of the Syrian civil war. The KRG sponsored the first meetings of the KNC in 2011 to address the Syrian crisis and what it meant to Kurds. Since 2011, the KNC has grown to include fifteen Kurdish political parties in Syria including the PYD. The KNC differs from the Syrian National Congress (SNC) because the KNC demands decentralization (as oppose to federalist aims) and autonomy from any Syrian government.

KDP: Acronym for the Kurdish Democratic Party. The KDP is one of the main political parties in Iraqi Kurdistan and is opposed by the PUK. The KDP was founded in 1946 during the collapse of the Kurdish Republic of Mahabad in Iran. The KDP started as and for many decades was a broad coalition of communist and socialist groups. During the First Persian War (the Iran/Iraq war) it repositioned itself as more of a national-ist and populist coalition with some social-democratic groups included.

Kongra-Gel: The name of the general Assembly of the KCK (and prior to that, the KKK). The Kongra-Gel has five subdivisions: political ideology, social services, political/international, military, and women's divisions.

KRG: Kurdish acronym for the Kurdistan Regional Government in Iraq. The KRG has a unicameral parliament known as the IKP (Iraqi Kurdistan Parliament). The KRG has both a president and prime minister that share executive and legislative powers. The President of the KRG is the commander-in-chief of the peshmerga forces. The city of Erbil (known in Kurdish as Hewler) is the capital of the KRG. The KRG governs about 8.5 million people spread over 15,000 square miles in northern Iraq. While the KRG was initially created after years of bloody fighting by a treaty signed by the Iraqi government in 1970, this treaty wasn't fully implemented until after the first Gulf War in 1992. The KRG was written into the new Iraqi constitution in 2005. There are still boundary disputes between the Iraqi government and the KRG, particularly as the KRG has annexed lucrative oil-fields south and east of Erbil.

Kurdistan: An Ill-defined region straddling Turkey, Syria, Iraq, and Iran composed of mostly Kurdish communities. Kurdistan is not internationally recognized. North Kurdistan is in Turkey, East Kurdistan is in Iraq and Iran, and West Kurdistan is in Syria.

KWU: The acronym for the Kurdish Women's Union. The KWU is part of the KDP and was founded in 1952. It has a strong impact on the KDP, especially around social services and economics.

Mahabad Republic: The Mahabad Republic (aka Republic of Kurdistan) was a short-lived independent Kurdish state situated in northern Iran from 1946-7. It was backed by the Soviet Union and was eventually crushed by the Iranian government when the USSR withdraw support.

MIT: Turkish acronym for *Milli İstihbarat Teşkilatı,* the National Intelligence Organization. MIT was founded in 1965. This is the governmental organization most responsible for coordinating the repression of the Kurds in Turkey today. In US terms, it is the equivalent of a combination of the FBI and CIA. The PKK and other Kurdish organizations supporting Kurdish rights and self-determination are tracked, suppressed, arrested, and killed by the MIT.

Newroz: New Year's Day, the most important holiday of the Kurds. This mid-March festival is often used as a political demonstration against Kurdish repression.

NCSROF: The acronym for the National Coalition for Syrian Revolutionary and Opposition Forces. The NCSROF started in 2012 to bring rebel armed groups into a coalition alongside strictly political opposition parties/organizations. The SNC is the largest partner in the coalition, controlling 22 of the 63 members of coalition. Their goal is to create an interim government, a truth and reconciliation committee to look into war crimes, and to be the "voice of opposition to the Assad regime" to the rest of the world. They also helped unify and amplify the Free Syrian Army (FSA).

Ottoman Empire: A massive empire that lasted for over six centuries and included the traditional homeland of the Kurds. The empire was dismembered after losing in World War I and a number of states were born out of the defeated empire, including Iran, Iraq, Syria, and Turkey.

Persian: Persian is a word for both a people and a language. Persians are non-arabic people (whom the Kurds are related to) mostly found in present-day Iran. Persian subgroups and languages can be found in such countries as: Iran, Tajikistan, Afghanistan, Turkey, Oman, Kuwait, Azerbaijan, and Uzbekistan.

Peshmerga: A Kurdish word that translates roughly as "those who confront death." Peshmerga has been the name of the Kurdish movements' fighting forces since 1921. Today, peshmerga is the official name of the KRG's armed forces. There are currently over a 100,000 men and women in the peshmerga armed forces in Iraq (of which, about 35,000 work inside the Iraqi National Armed Forces).

PJAK: Kurdish acronym for the *Partiya Jiyana Azad a Kurdistanê*, the Free Life Party of Kurdistan. PJAK is a large Kurdish militant and political organization in Iran that was founded in 2004. It is strongly aligned with the PKK. There is strong coordination and sharing of resources between the PKK and PJAK. PJAK is a member of the KCK.

PKK: Kurdish acronym for *Partiya Karkerên Kurdistani*, the Kurdistan Workers party, the Kurdish militant international organization.

PUK: Acronym for the Patriotic Union of Kurdistan. PUK is one of the main political parties in Iraqi Kurdistan and was founded in 1975. The KRG's current president, Fuad Massum, is a member of the PUK. PUK is a moderate socialist political coalition made up of five smaller leftist organizations.

PYD: Kurdish acronym for *Partiya Yekîtiya Demokrat*, the Democratic Union Party. PYD is a Syrian political party that started in 2003, is affiliated with the PKK, and is a member of the KCK.

Recep Tayyip Erdoğan: The current president of Turkey and the founder of the ruling Justice and Development Party (AKP). He was elected to president in 2014.

Rojava Canton: Any one of the three semi-autonomous regions in northern Syria. In late 2012, the KNC and PYD called for a Rojava Republic free of Syrian government control. By 2013, YPG/YPJ forces had liberated 9 cities and numerous villages in the north of Syria with a total population of about 3.5 million.

Rojava Confederation (AKA Rojava Republics): A confederation that consists currently of the three autonomous Rojava cantons: Cizîrê, Kobanî, and Efrin.

Salafist: A member of the conservative Sunni religious movement that seeks to emulate the earliest Muslims. Often associated with jihad.

SAVAK: An acronym for *Sāzemān-e Ettelā'āt va Amniyat-e Keshvar*, the Organization of Intelligence and National Security SAVAK was the Iranian secret police under the Shah, operating from 1957 – 1979. SAVAK is famous for both its brutality and its Western backing.

SNC: An acronym for the Syrian National Congress, which was formed in Istanbul in 2011. The SNC sought to be a coalition of oppositional groups, organizations, and political parties in Syria. Many of the founding members are Muslim Brotherhood in exile. Only one very small exile Kurdish party (the Kurdish Future Movement, which has split into two factions) joined the SNC. The SNC joined the National Coalition for Syrian Revolutionary and Opposition Forces (NCSROF) in 2012.

Shia: A minority sect of Islam. Shias (sometimes refered to as shiiites) believe that Mohommed's son-in-law and cousin Ali, as well as Ali's descendants (the Imams), are free from human sin.

Sunni: Sunni is the majority sect of Islam. Sunnis follow the teachings of the first four Caliphs after the Prophet Muhammad.

TEV-DEM: A shortening of *Tevgera Civaka Demokratîk*, the Movement for a Democratic Society. TEV-DEM is the political coalition of the Rojava area in Syria. In 2011, after massive protests against the Syrian regime, citizen groups and assemblies formed that were supported by the PYD and PKK. This coalition of groups formed into the TEV-DEM by late 2011. TEV-DEM sought to bring in people other than Kurds living in the region and had some success in getting Arabs, Christians,

Yezedi, Assyrians, and Turkmen to actively participate in the TEV-DEM councils.

Yezedi: A Kurdish monotheistic religious minority that has been targeted for complete destruction by ISIS. There are Yezedis in both Syria and Iraq.

YPG: A Kurdish acronym for *Yekîneyên Parastina Gel,* the Peoples' Protection Units. The YPG was founded in 2004 by the PYD but did not actually become active until 2012. The YPG is a coed militia that makes up the main fighting force for the Rojava region. There are about 45,000 to 50,000 women and men fighting in the YPG.

YPJ: Kurdish acronym for *Yekîneyên Parastina Jinê*, the Women's Protection Units. The idea for the YPJ appeared as early as 2006 but the YPJ did not become active until 2012. They are an armed, all-female militia, 10,000 strong, that alongside the YPG make up the main fighting force of Rojava.

Made in the USA
San Bernardino, CA
28 February 2015